From life crisis to lifelong learning

From life crisis to lifelong learning

Rethinking working-class 'drop out' from higher education

Jocey Quinn, Liz Thomas, Kim Slack,
Lorraine Casey, Wayne Thexton and John Noble

JOSEPH ROWNTREE
FOUNDATION

The **Joseph Rowntree Foundation** has supported this project as part of its programme of research and innovative development projects, which it hopes will be of value to policy makers, practitioners and service users. The facts presented and views expressed in this report are, however, those of the authors and not necessarily those of the Foundation.

Joseph Rowntree Foundation, The Homestead, 40 Water End, York YO30 6WP
Website: www.jrf.org.uk

Dr Jocey Quinn is Lecturer in Higher Education in the School of Education and Lifelong Learning, Exeter University.

Dr Liz Thomas is Senior Adviser for Widening Participation at the Higher Education Academy and Vice-President for Research and Publications with the European Access Network.

Kim Slack is Research Fellow in the Institute for Access Studies, Staffordshire University.

Lorraine Casey was a Research Officer in the Institute for Access Studies, Staffordshire University until November 2004.

Wayne Thexton is now an independent researcher, having previously worked as a Research Fellow in the Institute for Access Studies, Staffordshire University.

John Noble is a PhD Research Scholar working in the Institute for Access Studies, Staffordshire University.

ISBN 1 85935 412 2   (paperback)
ISBN 1 85935 413 0   (pdf: available at www.jrf.org.uk)

A CIP catalogue record for this report is available from the British Library.

Cover design by Adkins Design

Prepared and printed by:
York Publishing Services Ltd
64 Hallfield Road
Layerthorpe
York YO31 7ZQ
Tel: 01904 430033; Fax: 01904 430868; Website: www.yps-publishing.co.uk

Further copies of this report, or any other JRF publication, can be obtained either from the JRF website (www.jrf.org.uk/bookshop/) or from our distributor, York Publishing Services Ltd, at the above address.

Contents

Acknowledgements

With thanks to our expert partners: Hazel Knox, University of Paisley; Gerry McAleavy and Celia O'Hagan, University of Ulster; and Danny Saunders, University of Glamorgan.

Thanks also to the Joseph Rowntree Advisory Group for all their help: Steve Ingram, DfES; Veronique Johnston, Napier University; Stella Mascarenhas-Keyes, DfES; Veronica McGivney, NIACE; Louise Morley, Institute of Education, London; David Thompson, DfES; and Diane Reay, London Metropolitan University.

Thanks to the participant facilitators and to Jo Astley and Carmel Dennison of Staffordshire University.

Thanks also to Chris Goulden and Mark Hinman of the Joseph Rowntree Foundation.

Names of participants have been changed to protect their anonymity.

1 Introduction

'Drop out' and poverty

This report is part of the Joseph Rowntree Foundation's 'Ladders out of Poverty' programme. The traditional ladder out of poverty is education. Access to university education is seen as countering social exclusion and poverty, fostering local and national regeneration across the UK. Universities are trumpeted as playing 'a vital part in expanding opportunity and promoting social justice' (DfES, 2003a). Indeed, the Scottish Parliament established widening participation as 'Milestone 16' in progress towards a more socially just Scotland (Scottish Executive, 1999).

Universities are positioned within the 'poverty industry', among a raft of initiatives and institutions expected to respond to and compensate for those factors that help produce poverty, such as the decline of local industries. However, the assumption that higher education (HE) automatically produces escape from poverty and paths to social justice is challenged by the growing phenomenon of 'voluntary' withdrawal among young 'working-class' students. Such students are often climbing down the ladders offered to them. This is the focus of our study – not students who have failed, nor those who transfer across to other courses or institutions, but those who choose, seemingly of their own volition, to withdraw from university early.

How might we identify these working-class students when it is notoriously difficult to quantify class in any context, including HE? A recent international study of widening participation across ten countries concludes that:

> Whether a student is seen to belong to a low socio-economic group seems to depend on four main factors: income, occupation, geography and level of education … Nevertheless it can be argued that understandings of 'working class identity' as linked to lack of economic or cultural capital underlie all of these definitions of socio-economic status, even though identifying class is increasingly complex and contested. (Thomas and Quinn, 2003, pp. 82–3)

In our research on 'drop out', we decided to employ the definition of local, first-generation learner to identify students as working class. This is clearly not without problems, but research at an international level (for example, Knighton, 2002) has indicated that first-generation status is more indicative of educational disadvantage than parental occupation or income. Using this classification overcomes many of the difficulties of asking students to identify their own socio-economic status, while still capturing those who would have been deemed working class by more traditional indicators, such as coming from a low-income family or having parents in unskilled or manual occupations.

Data compiled by the Higher Education Funding Council for England (HEFCE) reveals wide institutional variations in student non-completion rates. Whereas some institutions retain all or virtually all of their students, other institutions (typically, former polytechnics who gained university status post 1992) retain just over half of their annual intake.

In the UK, unlike other nations, such as Sweden, we lack the statistical evidence to accurately measure working-class withdrawal overall. Nevertheless, existing performance indicators demonstrate rates of completion are generally lower at post-1992 universities (HESA, 2004). As these institutions attract more students deemed to be working-class because of their postcode or parental occupation in skilled manual, semi-skilled or unskilled occupations, this process has been constructed as 'drop out' and assumed to be a working-class 'problem'.

Working-class 'drop out' has been clearly defined as a policy priority across the UK. Redressing 'drop out' is seen as having a role in economic growth, employment, stability and social equality.

Widening participation and working-class 'drop out' in the UK

Although widening participation is a key policy imperative across the UK, devolution has created an increasingly complex picture. Common approaches include an emphasis on collaboration and partnership between higher education institutions (HEIs) and other sectors (particularly in England, Wales and Scotland) and payments to institutions to support retention of under-represented groups. Significant differences include the introduction of deferred top-up fees and maintenance grants in England and Northern Ireland.

Reaching the target of 50 per cent participation in higher education among those under 30 by 2010 is the cornerstone of the Government's widening participation policy. Such participation includes a broadening of the system to include HE courses located in further education (FE) colleges and foundation courses, as well as traditional three-year courses. Policy makers have grown increasingly concerned about working-class non-participation and non-completion and its effect on this target:

> The social gap in entry to HE remains unacceptably wide ... the
> proportion coming from lower-income families has not substantially
> increased. It means a waste of potential for individuals and for the
> country as a whole.
> (DfES, 2003a, p. 8)

In the UK, despite non-completion rates staying broadly the same since 1992 and
figures favouring well in comparison to other countries, improving student retention
still remains one of the Government's highest policy concerns:

> Non-completion is a waste of talent and resources and we expect HEIs to
> see what action they can take to help students. The Government expects
> all institutions to bear down on non-completion and in particular to work
> with those institutions with higher completion rates.
> (DfES representative, quoted in Tarleton, 2003)

Different policy contexts

Working-class 'drop out' is an issue across the UK. In Scotland, although 50 per cent
of school leavers now participate in HE (Scottish Executive Enterprise and Lifelong
Learning Committee, 2002), 'drop out' is perceived as a serious problem, with some
new universities with high working-class participation experiencing rates of 23 per
cent. In Wales, although 'widening access is high on the policy list' for the Welsh
Assembly (UUK, 2002, p. 104), there is great concern about the ability of universities
to attract and retain working-class students. In Northern Ireland, although 42 per cent
of the 18- to 21-year-old cohort progress to HE, participation in some areas is
'negligible' (UUK, 2002, p. 85) and 'drop out' is firmly on the policy agenda.

Recent statistical analysis of the probability of withdrawal for UK university students
indicated that non-completion was more probable for students from low-ranked,
occupationally defined social classes (Smith and Naylor, 2001) than for other
classes. Many assume that this is a matter of academic failure. However, research
indicates that a crude equation of academic ability with social class is not valid
(Johnston, 1997; NAO, 2002) and that the issue is far more complex.

In the most influential research on 'drop out' in the UK, Yorke (1997) identified the
five most significant reasons for student non-completion generally as: incompatibility
between the student and institution, lack of preparation for the higher education
experience, lack of commitment to the course, financial hardship and poor academic
progress.

Although Yorke himself does not emphasise the class dimension, these factors are more highly weighted towards working-class students, because of their lack of both cultural and economic capital, and their likely disadvantage in school education. Research conducted in Scotland for the Joseph Rowntree Foundation indicated it was the poorest students who were most likely to withdraw (Forsyth and Furlong, 2003). Class and poverty does matter in 'drop out' because it constructs the material inequalities that make it more difficult to survive and prosper as a student. However, these previous studies do not explain the high rate of working-class withdrawal or explore its broader implications. Our research explores the paradox that, even in universities offering high levels of support, in localities that have been subject to industrial decline and offer predominantly low-waged alternatives to study, working-class students are still leaving university early.

Working-class 'drop out' should not be constructed as inevitable: in practice, some working-class students will be highly successful. Moreover, voluntary early withdrawal exists among middle-class students too. Yet working-class 'drop out' confounds some of our most cherished assumptions about escapes from poverty. We need to understand why so many working-class students climb down the ladders offered to them.

The research

The overall goal of the research was both to understand the meanings and implications of 'voluntary' withdrawal among working-class students under 25 and to offer new perspectives and potential solutions. The focus here is on those who tend to disappear from view – working-class students who choose to leave before completion.

Ozga and Sukhnandan (1997) argue that retention research is based either on national statistical data or on isolated institutional studies. Either significant local impacts are lost or the focus remains narrow and parochial. Our aim was to provide a UK-wide focus for the research, rather than concentrating solely on one institution. Consequently, the research involved four post-1992 universities from England, Scotland, Wales and Northern Ireland, identifying them as part of their local and national communities, not as isolated entities. The universities were chosen because they were similar institutions that had all prioritised widening participation, but did have problems with retention. They all had strong links with their local communities and recruited heavily among local students.

The partner universities in this project are all in areas that have experienced a decline in traditional industries such as pottery, mining, shipbuilding, engineering and textiles. These localities experience significant problems of poverty and unemployment and each is commonly perceived as 'a gloomy area with social difficulties' (research participant).

Most major work on the relationship between class and HE has taken place in a metropolitan context, yet there are indicators that London should not be seen as the priority area for concern. Recent research from HEFCE on young participation in higher education demonstrates that:

> The growth in young participation in London has been particularly high ...
> In contrast low participation regions have seen little growth in participation.
> (HEFCE, 2005, p. 136)

Our research is important in moving beyond London to the provincial heartlands of the UK where very different cultures and questions may pertain.

The universities concerned have all targeted working-class students. They can all be seen as widening-participation institutions and they recruit heavily from their local areas. The following excerpt from one mission statement exemplifies the approach taken by these institutions:

> As an accessible learning community, we value inclusion and diversity and share the Government's commitment to increasing access and widening participation. We remain committed to ensuring that people from all backgrounds have the opportunity to study with us and that we encourage a wider social mix. We work to attract learners with a wide variety of previous life and educational experiences.

The latest available figures for all four institutions indicate that they exceed their benchmarks for recruitment for young full-time degree students from 'low' social classes (HESA, 2004).

Each university strives to provide student support and teaching and learning advice. For example, the following typical forms of support are offered in one university:

- mentoring schemes

- personal tutor scheme

- work bank – on-site employment agency for part-/full-time work and graduate work

- careers service

- chaplaincy service

- childcare provision

- counselling service

- disability service offering a range of activities/support to students (e.g. academic and domestic support worker service; specialist disability staff to offer advice, information and support from pre-enrolment through to graduation; help with organising additional examination arrangements; professional assessment of academic support needs and assistive technology; on-site diagnostic testing for dyslexia; specialist dyslexia tuition; support for deaf and hard-of-hearing students; and adapted, accessible rooms in halls of residence)

- student health services

- learning support

- student information centre/student guidance centre – the main first point of contact for students experiencing difficulties – students can access the guidance centre either in person or via the web to seek advice on any issue (finance, changing course, applying for hardship funds).

They have all conducted research and initiated projects to improve retention. Nevertheless, they all experience significant early withdrawal, even though they are based in areas experiencing serious local labour market difficulties. For example, in one institution, non-continuation of young entrants following their first year of entry reached 19.4 per cent in 2001/02, while the other three had levels of 12.9 per cent, 12.1 per cent and 10.3 per cent – all higher than the national average of around 7 per cent (HESA, 2004).

We focused on such universities rather than exploring more middle-class institutions with more national intakes, because they bring the question of voluntary 'drop out' into relief. Much research on class and higher education has stressed the alienation of the working-class student in the university environment. In theory, such new universities might be seen as more hospitable to working-class students, shielding them from withdrawal. Moreover temptations into the labour market, sometimes used as an explanation for leaving, do not so readily apply. Yet early withdrawal still exists: why?

Methodology

The research was conducted by a core team of six researchers originating from the Institute for Access Studies, Staffordshire University. A steering group of expert partners from each university enabled us to gain access to the institutions and their data.

The methodology we adopted addressed areas where existing research on early withdrawal was felt to be inadequate and we attempted to develop a more appropriate approach:

> There is a scarcity of data about the causes of non-completion by target group students.
> (UUK, 2002, p. 151)

One of the reasons is that those attempting to research early withdrawal have encountered methodological problems. Those who have used postal and telephone survey methods to explore student 'drop out' (for example, Johnes and Taylor, 1991; Davies and Elias, 2003) achieved a very low response rate. This led to difficulty in interpreting the findings and doubt about how representative they were.

We believed that 'drop out' was a complex and emotive issue, which needed exploring in depth. We wanted to unravel the meanings and impacts of 'drop out' for individuals, institutions and communities themselves, and in order to do so we needed our participants to help shape the terms and the process of the research. Consequently, a different qualitative and participative approach was necessary. Our research sought to maximise participation and attempted to involve ex-students using a range of qualitative methods.

The project began with research 'jury days' at each national location, organised via the steering group. Universities are increasingly expected to play a role in their community:

> HE has a critical role to play in the community, both as a social and
> cultural centre and as a community leader.
> (DfES, 2003a, p. 41)

We believed it was crucial to place universities in their local contexts and explore the perspectives of a range of local stakeholders on 'drop out' and its causes and impacts.

This was followed by in-depth interviews with 67 full-time undergraduate working-class students under 25 who have withdrawn early from the four universities over the past five years.

In three of the four institutional samples, there were more men than women (see Figure 1). This reflects national trends where young men are more likely to withdraw early from university than young women (HEFCE, 2005).

Although we did not aim to have mainly white participants, the overall sample contained only one minority ethnic student. This reflects the localities studied where ethnic minorities are not well represented. In Northern Ireland, for example, minority ethnic groups constitute only 1 per cent of the population. We do not claim that 'drop out' is only a 'white issue'. Although, overall, participation in HE is higher for minority ethnic working-class people than for white, there are many inequalities that the statistics on race and participation tend to hide, such as lack of access to elite institutions and subjects, institutional racism and marked differences across ethnic groups (see Connor *et al.*, 2004). When it comes to withdrawing early, the preliminary DfES figures discussed by Connor *et al.* (2004) suggest that:

Figure 1 Gender of participants by institution

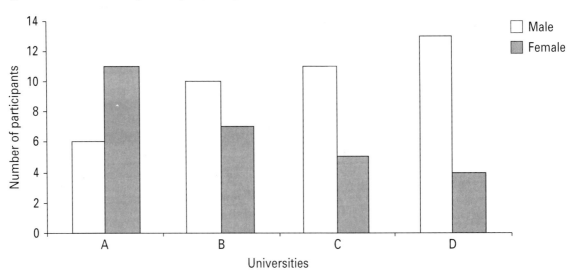

… non continuation figures are higher for Asian and Black than White students, but when allowances are made for differences by subject, entry qualifications and age (i.e. the usual HEFCE 'benchmark variables') young minority ethnic students on full time courses appear to do slightly better (continuation-wise) than expected.
(Connor *et al.*, 2004, p. 60)

Race is an issue in 'drop out', but there are many national variations. Our study is most useful in focusing on provincial, white, working-class young people and, in particular, on white men.

In doing so we are highlighting a group who are doing least well in educational terms and who tend to be ignored and marginalised:

… young women in England are 18 percent more likely to enter HE than young men. This inequality is more marked for young men living in the most disadvantaged areas and is further compounded by the fact that young men are less likely than young women to successfully complete their HE course and gain a qualification.
(HEFCE, 2005, p. 10)

Analysis of class based on 'use value' suggests that it is young, white, working-class people who are positioned as most 'redundant' in UK society, their labour no longer needed and they themselves not even possessing the cultural value that can attach to multiculturalism (Skeggs, 2004). Our strong focus on young, working-class, white men in disadvantaged provincial areas can therefore be seen as a strength of this study, and of particular interest to policy makers.

The findings of the research jury days and the interviews with students were interrogated in an international participative colloquium involving researchers, practitioners and policy makers. The colloquium also considered a set of specially commissioned international research papers exploring how 'drop out' was understood in other countries

The issue of flexibility and return to study emerged as particularly important. Consequently, we completed the study by interviewing university careers and employment services, and also conducted a small survey of those knowledgeable about university admissions processes.

Some methodological issues

It is important to contextualise early withdrawal and establishing a grounded picture was a crucial part of this research. Each of the four partner institutions hosted a 'research jury day' where the researchers heard evidence from a variety of sources including: working-class students still at the university, working-class students who had dropped out, lecturers and student support staff, employers, employment agencies, the voluntary sector and representatives from local communities about what they believe to be the meanings and consequences of 'drop out'. Counterparts of all the speakers – for example, other employers, other lecturers – were also involved in the day, to ask questions and take part in discussion.

Working-class withdrawal was placed, not in isolation, but in relation to local and national contexts, in order that the research team, before proceeding to the interview stage, could better understand its impact and implications.

The research jury days cannot claim to be a totally open method; the research team was making structural choices in whom we invited to speak (and whom we were able to get) and in turn those speakers were gatekeepers for many more perspectives. Since communities are so diverse, there were many voices 'experienced as absences', much as students who have dropped out are said to be.

In evaluative discussions following the event, the use of the term 'jury' was questioned as setting up connotations of judgement that might prevent some being willing to take part. However, for others, the notion of bearing witness and providing evidence was an important element of the process.

The jury days brought together not only the participants' own stories about 'drop out' but also the stories in currency about others, giving a sense of the cumulative and layering effect of the cultural narrative of 'drop out'. Their function was to uncover localised understandings of 'drop out' and explore the interconnections between the university, work and the community. By bringing together a range of participants who would rarely have entered into dialogue and by carefully structuring that dialogue, a wealth of challenging data was generated. In all, the research jury days have enabled 'drop out' to be explored and understood in a radically different way.

As explained previously, we used the definition of local first-generation learner as a proxy for 'working class' in gathering our sample of students who had withdrawn early. We understand 'working class' to be a highly heterogeneous category and the sample was, as expected, rich and diverse.

Gaining access to respondents is the persistent problem facing those who want to research students who have dropped out. We recognised this from the outset and created the role of the participant facilitator in each university to mediate between researchers and participants. These were to be students who had either dropped out themselves or were at risk of doing so. We believed that they would be able to communicate effectively with possible participants and encourage them to take part, using informal networks and contacts to create a snowball effect.

Although the participant facilitators did play an important role in contacting ex-students and arranging interviews, we did not feel the full potential of this methodological innovation was fulfilled. In practice, the participant facilitators tended to primarily use university data rather than informal means and, in some cases, they were hindered by their personal insecurities engendered by their own experience of dropping out. Greater support and better briefing could have helped redress this problem.

However, even for those who were most confident and persistent in using the university data, the facilitators faced some insuperable problems caused by the inaccuracy of the data provided by the universities involved. Many of the ex-students listed as under 25 were not, as the research team discovered when they came to interview them. Moreover, some had never been undergraduates or had not dropped out, raising serious concerns about university data collection and its use.

The team has therefore collected a set of data from ten middle-class students, which will prove valuable but is not used in this report.

Interviews were initially conducted by the research team on a face-to-face basis. However, many ex-students did not turn up for the appointments made by the facilitators, even in those universities that had offered financial incentives. Further interviews were conducted by telephone but contact also proved to be problematic and required some persistence on the part of the researchers. Despite some of the limitations of telephone interviews, the research team concluded that they were more realistic than expecting ex-students to return to a university from which they had dropped out.

Conclusion

Education is seen as a ladder out of poverty and universities as agents for local regeneration. However, many young working-class students are choosing to climb down the ladder and withdraw early. This has been identified as an important policy issue and a potential threat to widening participation in higher education, which is one of the UK Government's highest priorities. This research project is located in four post-1992 universities in disadvantaged provincial areas across England, Scotland, Wales and Northern Ireland. It uses a range of qualitative methods to explore the meanings and implications of such young working-class 'drop out', and to offer new perspectives and potential solutions.

2 Constructing 'working-class drop out' in the UK

Introduction

It is important to recognise that 'working-class drop out' is a construct that sets the frame for how early withdrawal is understood and experienced in the UK. In this chapter, we briefly outline how this emerges in policy discourse and in popular media. We then explore the ways in which it functions as a popular 'story' about working-class people, arguing that it is one of the most recent manifestations of the way working-class people are consistently positioned as inherently 'flawed' and 'lacking'(see Quinn, 2004).

Retention as a moral imperative

Attendance at university has become almost a prerequisite for citizenship for young people in the UK. The White Paper on *The Future of Higher Education,* for example, asserts:

> HE also brings social benefits ... there is strong evidence that graduates
> are more likely to be engaged citizens.
> (DfES, 2003a, p. 59)

Retaining students has been positioned by policy makers as a moral imperative for institutions. Non-retention is seen as 'setting students up to fail' and as 'unacceptable' (DfES, 2003b). HEFCE has been tasked with 'bearing down on non-completion' and on those institutions that allow it to happen (DfES, 2003b).

UK policy on student 'drop out' from post-compulsory education is dominated by a narrow conception of lifelong learning and withdrawal, with the focus on linear progression and completion. Students are generally expected to complete their studies within a fixed and predetermined time, and the primary objective is to retain students on the courses on which they initially enrolled.

This view of retention tends to pathologise new constituencies of learners, perhaps for being poorly prepared for university or even for lacking academic ability.

'Drop out' as a lack of moral fibre

While remaining in university is cast as a virtue, deciding to leave is popularly portrayed as a lack of moral fibre. Longden (2003) identifies the following labels: 'failure', 'drop-out', 'non achievement' and 'wastage'.

Such negative language is apparent in recent media articles relating to non-completion. For example, some recent headlines in the *Times Higher Education Supplement* include:

> You can't count on the *carefree*
> (Times Higher Education Supplement, *29 March 2002*)

> Paisley calls for probe of *quitters*
> (Times Higher Education Supplement, *4 April 2003*)

> UEL takes steps to tackle first year *failure* rate
> (Times Higher Education Supplement, *12 December 2003*)

> Plea to invest in stopping *dropouts*
> (Times Higher Education Supplement, *7 May 2004*)

Our interview participants were well aware how this label could be internalised and also used to position them in the minds of others:

> When you 'drop out' of uni there's a stigma. You're a university 'drop out'.
> (Male)

'Drop out' as a 'story' about working-class people

The research, in particular the jury days, revealed how 'drop out' functions as a pervasive 'story' about working-class students, which circulated widely in the community, within institutions and among policy makers. The story is that working-class cultures and choices are 'wrong' and 'drop out' is just another way in which working-class people demonstrate their failure to succeed. This story is not harmless; it shapes the way the issue of voluntary withdrawal is understood and frames the kinds of actions that are proposed in relation to it. A useful analogy can be made with domestic violence. At one time, the dominant cultural narrative was that violence in the home was a private matter and the woman's fault. Only by replacing this with another narrative and way of seeing could appropriate actions be taken by the authorities. 'Drop out' requires a similar cultural rethinking.

Although 'drop out' is increasingly recognised as complex and multifaceted, it is still dominantly conceptualised as a path that can be traced, however winding, with problems that can be rectified through institutional change or better student support. However, we would argue that this path can lead us only so far. The research jury days highlighted 'drop out' as a popular story that in itself has an element of self-fulfilling prophecy. They revealed that 'drop out' has a life of its own. This narrative creates an expectation that, in this area and in these institutions, many students will 'drop out'. Actions then model those expectations.

For communities such as those in this research, working-class culture remains the reference point for very many people. Although that culture itself is not homogeneous, it still generates working-class affinities and identifications. Middle-class identity may be increasingly normalised within the wider national sphere, but the unspoken norm in large tranches of these localised communities remains working-class. Narratives of masculine employment still circulate as nostalgia and desire in these locations, and interact in complex ways with new narratives of progression, such as that of the mass participation of women in HE. 'Drop out' is therefore positioned firmly within the paradoxes of contemporary working-class culture.

In the past, working-class people have largely accessed higher education through part-time provision and the polytechnic sector. The expectation that they will be full-time university students at 18 or of there being a local 'university' to go to is a very new, essentially post-1992, phenomenon in the UK. Although the notion that university is an alien landscape retains some potency and access has not proportionally increased the participation of working-class students, expansion of numbers means that it has also become part of the normal expectation for many young working-class people.

For the universities in this study, working-class participation can be as high as 70 per cent of all students. Many of these students are local and the university has been a part of their everyday world growing up, with classmates and family members regularly attending. These are not ivory towers and these are not the 'scholarship boys' of yesteryear; this is the university as commonplace. For many people, these new universities are not thought of as 'real' universities but as 'ex-polys'.

While this new worldview helps to make university seem more accessible, it allows that university might be a flawed and unsatisfactory experience, and that 'drop out', rather than being unthinkable, is a possibility entertained from the outset. This is not to say that high hopes and idealistic visions do not exist or that they are never fulfilled. Indeed working-class students can be the most motivated and successful of students, drawing on the sustaining networks of working-class family and friends. Moreover, these universities provide them with many excellent educational opportunities. However 'university drop out' has become engrained in the ways in which working-class identity is currently portrayed and understood.

Although 'drop out' is certainly not unknown among middle-class students and at elite institutions, this research is particularly interested in how the notion of 'drop out' is becoming entwined with working-class identity and with 'new' universities. It has become a new facet of positioning working class as a 'spoilt identity' (Reay and Ball, 1997), an identity that is understood in terms of lack, as being in error and prone to failure.

Access to HE has not dismantled class, it has produced new stories of lack and failure, channelling working-class students into the lower tiers of an increasingly stratified system and also anticipating that they will not stay the course. Skeggs (1997) has demonstrated how classed stories ignore the positive in working-class culture and interpret what may be rational life decisions as symptoms of working-class unreliability and fecklessness. We argue that the popular story of 'working-class drop out' adds a new twist to this familiar picture.

'Drop out' and boys' underachievement

As discussed in Chapter 1, participation in higher education is lower for young men than for women, particularly in disadvantaged areas outside London. Of those who do enter, a higher proportion withdraw early than do young women.

Overall, participation in higher education among working-class minority ethnic men is proportionately high. It is young white men who are causing policy makers most concern (HEFCE, 2005). In Northern Ireland, this is particularly true of young Protestant men living in zones of disadvantage.

Early withdrawal by young white men has been strongly linked to boys' underachievement at school level, with 'drop out' seen as a natural outcome of what is believed to be boys' lack of motivation and forward planning and their susceptibility to peer group pressure (*Times Higher Education Supplement*, 2005, p. 21).

The classed story of 'drop out' is also a gendered one and those who 'lack' the most are young white men.

Conclusion

We cannot understand 'drop out' without understanding the framework in which it is placed and the judgements that surround it. Policy makers have cast retention and the uninterrupted completion of their degree by students as an absolute moral imperative for institutions. When students withdraw early, institutions are therefore deemed to have failed and are punished accordingly. The student's decision to leave early is never portrayed as a rational or even positive one, but as the outcome of a lack of moral fibre and a propensity to quit. 'Drop out' is seen as just the latest indicator of what is 'wrong' with the working class, as a foregone conclusion, because they lack the will and the ability to succeed, particularly if they are young, male and white. All these attitudes and judgements help to shape the expectations and actions of students, institutions and communities, and create a story of early withdrawal, which can be read only in terms of inevitability, failure and disappointment. We now want to use our research findings to write the story in a more productive way.

3 Reasons for leaving university: exploring the meanings of 'drop out'

Introduction

As we have seen in Chapter 2, early withdrawal from university is strongly framed in terms of lack and failure. But how do students understand it? Our research allowed us to explore the meanings of withdrawal as interpreted by the students themselves, rather than by policy makers or institutions, drawing on the interviews with 67 participants. The pattern of withdrawal in our study mirrored the findings of other retention research (for example, Yorke, 1997; Thomas, 2002), which see students as most likely to leave in their first year. Most of our participants had left in the first year with half of these leaving in their first semester. Although only one participant had made it to their third year, 13 had returned to university for a second year before ultimately leaving. Our analysis indicated that the reasons for leaving were complex and involved a range of factors. In this chapter, we will chart these factors and explore their meanings.

Being on the right course

Our participants had been enrolled on a range of courses, from the more traditionally academic such as social science to the more vocational such as nursing. There were gendered aspects to their choice of subjects with more males choosing subjects such as engineering and computer studies, and more females entering subjects such as business and marketing (see Table 1).

A distinction was made by students between being prepared for university and being prepared for the course they had chosen. Indeed, choosing the wrong course was given as the main reason for leaving by many of those involved in the research.

Almost without exception, students felt that they had made poorly informed subject choices. The process of choosing a university and a course was 'rushed', particularly for those who entered via Clearing, and left many leafing through a prospectus with no real sense of what they should be looking for other than they thought it would be 'interesting'. However, with little guidance from family, university or schools, the reality of the course often proved different to expectations. Families provided support but it was undirected support without a reserve of knowledge about HE to draw on. Families were happy for them to go but often equally as happy for them to withdraw:

Table 1 Courses followed by students by institution and by gender

Male	Female
University A	
Business analysis	Nursing (2)
Human resource management	Social science (2)
Media studies	Business
Film	Computer multimedia
Social science	
Computer networking (2)	
Computer engineering	
Computer games	
University B	
Energy and environment	Combined studies (2)
Humanities and social studies	BA in drama
Theatre and history	Sports studies (2)
Forensic science	Early years in education
Electrical engineering	Police science
Business	Social science
Media technology	
Business and information	
Theatre and history	
University C	
Computer science (2)	Law
Engineering	Business (2)
Sports studies (3)	Business management
Forensic engineering	Marketing
Crime and deviance	
Business (2)	
University D	
Computer studies (7)	Computer studies (3)
Building surveying	
Electronics and software	
Environmental health	
Computer multimedia	
Engineering	

> Again I didn't really know what I was going into because the prospectus
> didn't really give me that much of a clue. I know it was a new course, but I
> just feel that if they had told me what the exact things were then maybe I
> wouldn't have picked it.
> (Male)

Other students had chosen a course that they thought, or were advised, would be
relatively 'loose' in the sense of providing a wider choice of job options. However,
once on the course, they failed to see any link with a future career. While subjects
such as medicine have low rates of 'drop out' nationally, partly because of highly
supported middle-class intake, and also because the trajectory forward is clear,
others have less defined outcomes and therefore need to provide different forms of

validation to the student. This also involves the student in determining where they can best fit. It seems working-class students had not had the opportunity to develop those tools of self-assessment that are often well honed in a middle-class environment and that enable students to place themselves effectively and reap the benefits.

The level of commitment and motivation students experienced was limited by the extent to which they felt they were on the wrong course. Some students were unsure of their choice even before they arrived at university, and this impacted on their settling-in process, both academically and socially. For others, the realisation was more gradual.

Although a number of students found that they were unable to change to a different course because they were too far into the academic year, many did not enquire about other options such as studying part time simply because they were unaware they existed. While some felt that they would not have chosen to continue studying part time because of the extended time commitment required, others felt that this would have been a viable option if it had been suggested to them at the time.

Sarah's story

Sarah was the first person in her family to go to university. She was keen because she was told at school that's what people should do to get qualifications leading to a good job, and most of her friends went either to college or university. She didn't know what she wanted to study but eventually chose multimedia and web design, and she lived at home while attending university.

Sarah attended college before going on to university and felt that college lecturers gave far more help and support to their students than university lecturers did:

> You don't want to bother the lecturer because we don't think they care.

Sarah described the difficulties of sometimes not understanding lectures but not wanting to be the person to say so in front of the class. She also said that sometimes two lecturers teaching on the same course held conflicting views, which was confusing for the student:

> It was up to us to flag up problems but … nobody wants to be seen as the one who doesn't understand.

Continued

Sarah expected university to be different from college but did not expect it to be so difficult to ask for help. She reflected that part of her difficulty lay in the fact that she had chosen the wrong path and, if she could have turned the clock back, she would have chosen what her 'heart told her to do' rather than what she was advised. She also said that, once she was at university, she was too scared to ask for the help she needed:

> Someone to listen to ... is not a big thing to ask from a university.

She suggested that students should be made aware that there is someone willing to listen to problems other than the lecturers. She felt that universities should be more aware that people are scared to come forward with problems:

> They can cover their backs by saying we have got a noticeboard that says there's a counsellor, but that's not the same as somebody coming into class and saying we are here if you need to speak to us and you can come in confidence – it is nothing to be ashamed of. You are just a number. I am a statistic of somebody that has dropped ... Nobody realised there was anything wrong and no one asked ... The doctor was the first person I spoke to about the problem and she was the only one that said 'I understand'.

Sarah concluded:

> University is not the ideal that it is portrayed to you by the media, by the university, and by the school.

Academic culture shock

The transition from school or college to university was problematic for many students, even for those who had attended a summer school to familiarise young people with their local university:

> We weren't prepared for the transition between school and university and I went to a thing called a summer school in there as well. We were in a group of about 16 people and I thought, it's all right it is just like school. That gives you a false impression, the fact that you were in a small class and you had a teacher and then when I went to university there were 300 of us sitting in a lecture hall.
> (Female)

A number of factors were implicated in this. The combination of an increased workload and more freedom offered the opportunity to 'cop out' and fall behind. Students who felt they had 'coasted through' school and college suddenly experienced difficulties at university. This was not only unexpected, it also severely dented confidence in their ability to progress onto subsequent years of their degree course. This was frequently experienced as an increasing sense of loss of control:

Researcher:	What sort of things led up to you leaving, what sort of triggered it off?
Male interviewee:	No support, too much of a heavy workload, thinking that I was losing control in everything that I was studying.

Loss of confidence also affected their willingness or even ability to seek support.

Teaching and learning

The change in teaching and learning styles involved in the transition from school or college to university can prove problematic. Although students felt that they were 'warned' of this prior to entering HE, for many the extent of this change was something they were unprepared for in reality:

> I knew it would be a different atmosphere at university. It was a totally different world to college. They did give help but it wasn't the same. I'd go to a lecture, they would teach me and that would be it. You can't have any kind of a one-to-one … I had too much work and I didn't know how I was going to manage.
> (Female)

A number of students felt that they were unsure of whether to listen or take notes during lectures for example, or how to structure and plan their work. Many were not aware of specific advice and guidance available to help them to develop these skills:

> I just felt like I was out there, and I was on my own and there were not a lot of people who could help me in any way.

Furthermore, effective formative assessment and feedback was lacking to help them progress.

> There was some work that I felt I was doing enough in but I wasn't really getting the marks for it. Most of the class agreed they weren't getting a clear indication as to what was required for it.
> (Male)

> At college you get continuous assessments but it wasn't like it was at university. It's like – take this and go away, do your research and write 10,000 words. In college I was quite bright and I always finished my work weeks before the semester finished. At university I often thought – oh God, where am I going, what is happening here?
> (Male)

A distinction was evident between those students who said they liked studying in general but not studying the course they were on, and those who felt that 'the student life is not for me', expressing a preference for more practical, job-related learning:

> I think this is personal, or the type of person I am. When I was doing this degree it was like you learn how to make a cup software wise, but there is no purpose to it, there's no reason. Now I learn to make a cup and then I make 50 of them at work and the boss said this is fantastic I didn't know you could do that. And I have improved the time. And you are using it straight away and getting feedback.
> (Female)

Larger class sizes created problems in adjusting, engendering feelings of 'being lost' and 'faceless'. Furthermore, the high student-to-staff ratio restricted their ability to approach lecturers:

> They mixed classes, there was music technology and sound technology, and we were all together and there was just too big a group to have a more personal tutoring.
> (Male)

The quality of the relationships between staff and students varied significantly. Many students believed that they didn't really have any relationship with teaching staff at all. Teaching staff were often perceived as 'unapproachable':

> At university you have large groups, lots of people in one lecture. At college there are only about 25 people and you all get to know each other. The lecturer knows you. Everything is fine. Here the lecturer doesn't even know if you walk past him. He doesn't even know if you are a student. It makes it hard.
> (Female)

It was often difficult to make contact with staff and this was particularly problematic for students living at home and/or working, as they were restricted in their ability to wait around on campus.

Certain subjects appeared to be more problematic in terms of fostering feelings of isolation in students, for example, courses related to computer science. Online information systems and electronic learning environments, where all information on course materials, timings and locations is only available electronically, can increase feelings of alienation in new students who are unsure if they are accessing the correct information during a period frequently perceived as 'rushed' and confusing.

Academic struggle

Students struggling in their first year frequently assessed their position and decided that they would be unable to cope with higher-level academic work in subsequent years. In this situation, continuation represented a further waste of time or renewed/ increased effort that they felt unable to sustain:

> The course was really hard. I'd do my assignments and I was struggling. I went to the library and worked away, but I just found that no matter how much I studied I just couldn't get my head around it. It was too hard. I wouldn't be able to carry on. I just started to ask myself questions about continuing. I really studied hard but it didn't seem to make much difference. I would never get top marks.
> (Male)

Students entering university from FE in the third year of their course appeared to find the transition particularly problematic. While some lecturers appeared aware of the difficulties this involved and took steps to facilitate students' integration, others were less aware:

> I think he understood that most people come from college and there were differences in the way people were taught. He advised us how to go about taking notes and then looking at his notes. I found that very helpful. Other lecturers didn't go about it that way.
> (Female)

Many students had been repeating modules they had failed in previous years in addition to current coursework and this proved very difficult to cope with.

Student support

Although it was clear from the research jury days that institutions were providing high levels of student support, this had had little impact on our participants. A general lack of awareness and clarity in relation to both academic and more general student support was evident. Some were not aware any support was available; some had a vague idea but no meaningful sense of where or how to access it. Most were not able to identify the kind of support they most needed:

> We got the induction at university at the beginning and there was some talk about it, but we were never really told who to go to or where to go to, never entirely sure just what I could do if I needed help.
> (Male)

> We were told that there was a study helper kind of person if we were ever having any trouble in classes we could go to them. I was never told who it was, so if I ever needed I wouldn't know where to find them.
> (Male)

Many students expressed reluctance to avail themselves of support services, both in relation to academic support or more general support. They did not see themselves as the type of person the service was intended for, or felt embarrassment, shame and fear of 'looking like an idiot'.

Furthermore, students who felt they lacked any relationship with teaching staff were understandably hesitant to approach them about accessing further support. For example, one student had contacted administrative staff rather than one of his/her tutors to tell them they were thinking of leaving. This meant they were simply instructed on the technicalities of leaving rather than offered support.

There were also examples of students struggling academically who sought guidance from teaching staff and received little or no support:

> *Researcher:* When you became really stressed out, who did you go and see?
>
> *Interviewee (female):* I went to see the course tutor. I had tears. He just seemed to think it would be better for me to go.
>
> *Researcher:* Did he offer you any advice or support? Did he tell you about anywhere that you could go to get help?
>
> *Interviewee:* No my course tutor didn't. One of my other tutors said there would be help available but we were never really told about that. I don't think a lot of people were aware of that.

Although every institution offered some form of learning support, students regarded it as a thing apart and not as integrated into their everyday curriculum and classroom.

In some instances, practical support (e.g. for disabled students) was not available.

Noel's story

Noel comes from a working-class background and his parents were keen for him to go to university. His elder sister went to university and most of his friends also went on to university. Since his schooldays, he'd always wanted to do so. He chose his university because it offered electronic and software engineering, and also because it wasn't too far away from his home town. He had good relationships with other students and shared a house with some student friends:

> If I didn't go in one day or I missed a class I wouldn't see as many people, I'd miss the crack. The boys would come home and tell me what I'd missed. It made me want to go in.

Continued

Within a short time Noel realised he had chosen the wrong course:

> The first real experience you have of seeing what is done coursewise is when you actually start university. At the open days there are no real examples of work to show you ... Whenever people go on open days from school they're just happy to be out of school and they don't really know what to ask.

Noel withdrew at the start of the second semester:

> I just wasn't happy. I felt I was just wasting my life. There was no point in me just sitting there and getting into more debt when I could be at home working ... I made up my mind at that stage that I wanted to study architectural technology instead.

Noel spoke with the course director and he explained the options open to him and also helped him fill out the forms to register on the course of his choice for the following year:

> I told my friends. They weren't happy, they wanted me to stay. Mom and Dad were all right but they did want me to stick the first year out. I just thought there was no point in doing it ... Whenever you tell anybody you are leaving they just think you are a waster. It wasn't too bad for me because I was coming back.

Noel returned the following year to study architectural technology and management.

A sense of belonging

Developing a sense of belonging within an institution is clearly implicated in student retention (Thomas, 2002). Even new universities can be perceived as alien and middle-class, while at the same time not inspiring great respect among working-class students. For local students in particular, familiarity may breed contempt. Establishing a level of social and academic 'fit' proved to be problematic for many of the students involved in the research.

Universities were defined by one student as 'A place for people to meet, where friendships are made'. Developing new friendships facilitates integration and peer support can be a key factor in a student's decision to continue studying or withdraw.

A number of students experiencing difficulties academically were advised by their personal tutors to work in groups to support each other. However, this had sometimes proved unsuccessful because many students appeared to mix with others of a similar academic level:

> Yes I made friends … The ones I made friends with most were the same as me. They found some of the coursework was difficult.
> (Male)

For some students it proved difficult to become involved socially. Those who feel they are on the wrong course and who express lower levels of commitment to studying may have similar feelings about committing to new friendships and social activities. Social life was not easy even for those who desired it; some, particularly women, spoke of making a friend rather than friends, having meals alone and the difficulty of becoming part of a group.

Part-time and local students can experience barriers to social involvement (e.g. time on campus and transport difficulties) and, while some students who remained living in the family home expressed less desire to be involved in the social side of university, others regretted that they had been unable to move away to university, feeling that they had missed out on the 'real' student experience:

> … the people who lived there *[university]* were part of the environment, whereas I felt like a bit of an outsider. Even though I lived around here and it was my town. I felt like an outsider compared to the other people who were there.
> (Female)

Local students and part-time students are in theory able to access support from their existing friendship groups and family. In reality, this may not always be the case. Students whose friends have not entered HE may find that withdrawing confirms expectations in that 'all my mates were expecting me to quit anyway'.

Students whose old friends have also gone to university may be reluctant to discuss problems they are experiencing personally because:

> They *[their friends]* had done it and they succeeded. I didn't mention that I was struggling with the course or even talk about my thoughts of leaving.
> (Female)

Alternatively, relationships with old friends may suffer because of lack of contact:

> … the friendships went downhill because I was never with them.
> (Male)

Non-university commitments

'Non-university commitments' refers both to practical, time-consuming commitments, such as caring for family members or undertaking paid employment, and to social and emotional commitments. The latter could be as weighty or have similar negative impacts on continuation as more visible pressures. Furthermore, it is not always the simple existence or lack of particular social relations that can support or inhibit continuation. Rather, it may be access to those relations at key times during the student experience:

> Sometimes, when I did the foundation course, I didn't enjoy it, but then I'd go back to my room and I'd have a laugh with my mates again. When I wasn't living in halls and I had a bad lesson I'd just mope around for five hours until my next lecture.
> (Male)

Not all students worked in paid employment during their studies, but those who did framed it in one of two ways. On the one hand, there was talk of this being an energy- and time-sapping strain. On the other hand, simultaneous study and employment could be experienced as a positive approach to university life – it could open up alternative friendship circles or provide more stimulating experiences. At the time of leaving, it could provide support in preventing the individual from suddenly facing a great gap where study once was:

> *Researcher:* Were you working? Was that a commitment?
>
> *Interviewee (female):* Yes. I had a part-time job in Safeway – just working in the cash office. It got to the stage that when I wasn't going to university so much I did more hours at Safeway just to cover the day. I wasn't even turning up for university towards the end.

Financial pressures

Although few students cited finance as the ultimate reason for leaving early, it was an ever-present issue for most participants. Poverty was something that they had had to learn to live with and that shaped decisions such as studying and living at home:

> I wanted to stay at home; even though I got a student loan and stuff like that it is not enough money to live on so I did want to say at home.
> (Male)

The notion of having to undertake a financial struggle through the university years seemed to be implicitly accepted. Nevertheless, having to support themselves clearly contributed to the pressures they faced and resulted in time gaps, which they struggled to fill:

> It was hard, especially when lecturers said I had to do things by the next day. I'd have to do it after work but I didn't finish work until after 11 o'clock three or four nights a week.
> (Male)

> Also money was an issue. I could only fit in a few days at work. A lot of the time I found it hard to keep up with studies because I was working as well.
> (Male)

These findings concur with those of Van Dyke and Little (2002) who found that most students had accepted debt as 'normal', but that working-class students worked longer hours to cope with their financial pressures.

Many experienced their study as a serious drain on limited family resources. Thus leaving became an act of responsibility to the family as a whole:

> I think if I am honest if the financial side had been better for me I would probably have stayed there because I did enjoy the course but there was always pressure on my family to give me money and that is what made it harder to stay on the course, so I thought 'I will ditch this'.
> (Male)

Personal responsibility

The responsibility for the student leaving early was often attributed both internally and externally. Some acknowledged having the wrong 'attitude' in entering into university study but also called for institutional change:

Researcher:	Do you think anything could have been done to make you stay?
Interviewee (male):	If I had gone into it with a better attitude and done the work for myself. I am used to coasting through things. That's what I did at college and at school. I did the minimum amount of work needed to get through. At university, because there was no one there to tell me what to do and I had to do it for myself, I started to lag behind.
Researcher:	Do you think you would have stayed with it in a more disciplined environment?
Interviewee:	Yes, that would have suited me better probably.

There were occasions when students admitted that no amount of student support or any form of intervention would have inspired continuation. The fundamental desire to stay had been absent. This is not to suggest that a return to study would be impossible, but rather that the time and the subject were simply not right:

Interviewee (male):	There seemed no point to me coming here every day because I wasn't really interested in it.
Researcher:	The modules that you failed – do you think anybody could have done anything to help you?
Interviewee:	No, it was me. I just lost interest in the modules. Looking back on it I just wasn't trying to understand it. I had lost interest. I believed it wasn't for me and I didn't want to do it.

Student drift

Student drift is the gradual process by which some students' engagement with a university will end. This is typically understood in terms of a waning attendance at lectures, seminars and so on, which is often not recognised or commented on by the HEI staff:

> It had been building up for some time. I gradually started to go to classes less and less. There would be weeks that I didn't go, then I would turn up, speak to people, say I was embarrassed because I hadn't gone. Eventually, after the half-term break, I just didn't go back.
> (Female)

Researcher:	Tell me about the process by which you left?
Interviewee (male):	It was gradual and my attendance dwindled out. It wasn't an abrupt end, it was gradual. I started thinking about the options. As I attended some of the classes my mind became more made up and I realised it wasn't for me.

From the student perspective, it is easy to view the experience or existence of drift as a bad one – perhaps symbolic of institutions that 'don't care'. However, for some students, this allows an unforced decision to be made regarding choosing to discontinue study.

The following extract could be termed 'drift incorporated'. What stands out here is the student's own practically inactive response to gentle warnings about low attendance and the significance of their view of time:

Researcher:	When did you leave?
Interviewee (male):	Well, I think once the second year started a few months into it, I was going to most of the lectures at the beginning, but gradually I was falling away from it, I was just getting so fed up with certain subjects – maybe two or three out of four – I was really not enjoying, so I was not turning up very often for them or not really bothering, so that was one of the things.

Researcher: Did anybody sort of notice this? Any of the lecturers? Did anyone follow you up?

Interviewee: Not really, apart from maybe saying 'well you are falling behind a bit here' or 'you had better watch as you are falling behind', that was it. I can't remember if I got any letters through about it. It didn't go on over a long period, it was maybe about a month, or two months, then I just fell away from it completely after that.

Here, a month or two of drift is not seen to be a long time. However, in the case of a modular framework of study, for example, this could easily equate to a third or half of scheduled contact time for a module. This may suggest that drift can all too often go unrecognised, not only by the HEI, but also by the student.

Gender differences

Gender did appear to have an impact on reasons for leaving early as well as on choices of subject, although this was rarely explicit.

Gender had an impact on the process of socialisation. Young men found it easier to take advantage of social opportunities such as student bars than women did. However, this sometimes did not work to their advantage:

Interviewee (male):   I didn't have to be in lectures that often.

Researcher: What did you do with the time?

Interviewee: Sometimes we went to the library or worked on a problem on the computers, but nine times out of ten we just went to the bar.

Young men did seem to find it more difficult to admit to difficulties, particularly if their peers were not willing to speak out:

We were doing programming, I just couldn't understand it. My friends found it a bit iffy too but nobody would say anything so I didn't want to stand out. In the end they got to grips with it but I never did.
(Male)

They also seemed more reluctant to seek out student support and more fearful of 'looking like an idiot'.

Although our participants were under 25, young women sometimes had caring responsibilities for children or elderly parents, which added to the problems they faced in negotiating time and contact with lecturers.

The gendered nature of the labour market also had an impact. Young men exhibited nostalgia for the secure patterns of traditional industry and felt themselves pulled towards the remaining opportunities that existed:

> What I've got now I keep telling myself if I hadn't went to university I could have learned a trade and be earning good money.
> (Male participant, research jury day)

Stereotypical attitudes to young, white, working-class men as being rough and even dangerous, but at the same time weak and feckless, had had an impact on their educational progress. Sometimes it diverted them from the educational path that might have led to success, as with this student who was encouraged to drop maths for engineering and ultimately found his university course too boring to continue:

Researcher:	Were you encouraged to go to university from the sixth form?
Interviewee (male):	No, I don't think my background helped. I came from *[area C]*, as you probably know it has a bad reputation, I was an outsider. There was a parents' evening. I was doing A level maths. I was good at maths, I got a B in it. The maths teacher turned up and said he didn't think I suit maths because mathematicians are clever people. I sat with my jaw at the floor and thought fine. Was he saying I didn't suit being a clever person?
Researcher:	So you think you brought this stereotype with you?

Interviewee:	Yes. It sounds pathetic but my nickname was 'scary Pete', they all thought I was a bit psychotic. I had been in a rough area. I was a bit rough at the time so they didn't exactly like me.

However, we do not agree with the prevalent view that young working-class men lack the correct 'learning dispositions' (*Times Higher Educational Supplement*, 2005). There were many instances when young men had demonstrated enthusiasm for informal learning:

> All the way through school I was interested in gadgetry and electronics, so I decided that would be the best course for me.
> (Male)

> Music was my big thing; I was really into that in a big way.
> (Male)

The learning they were interested in was not taken seriously and they were often given poor careers advice, which took them in the wrong direction:

> I told them I wanted to make films for a living but they told me I'd never be able to do that. They made me tick boxes on a computer. The number one jobs the computer came up with were stonemason, police officer and mechanic.
> (Male)

On entering university, they could be alienated by pedagogic methods that were rigid and non-participatory and, ultimately, they became disillusioned and dropped out:

Researcher:	How did you find the teaching methods?
Interviewee (male):	Some cases good, some cases bad. One module was mainly practical experience – that one was more interesting. It was better than having your head in a book and being dictated to. I don't feel that's the right way to learn.

In many cases, they left university in an attempt to rekindle their original interests, demonstrating considerable persistence and belying the image of young, white, working-class men as the ultimate 'quitters':

> I'm making a Western set in Glasgow. My friend and I wrote it and shot it on video, now we're trying to set up as a limited company and get Lottery funding.
> (Male)

Conclusion: 'drop out' as a rational act and a learning experience

For some students in our study, 'drop out' was a non-choice, in that they drifted into it or initiated it rather than do exams or assignments they felt they would fail. However, for the majority, it can be perceived as a rational decision in response to a set of circumstances that made study at that time and place unproductive for them. However, because of the way it was managed by institutions and presented to students as a dead end, withdrawing was largely experienced as disempowering. This was true even when it was simultaneously a relief, 'a burden taken off my back'. Choosing to leave early became 'dropping out' with all its connotations of fecklessness and failure. However, 'drop out' can also be seen as a learning experience. With hindsight, participants were now aware of what they *should* have done at the time; such as choosing a course more carefully, finding out more detailed information on course content, being more aware of less explicit information contained within a prospectus, joining clubs or societies and seeking specific help or advice and guidance. They also point to the necessity for institutional changes, such as more accurate information about courses, more opportunities for peer support and group work, more integrated learning support within the curriculum – particularly at an early stage, better systems of personal tutoring, more targeted access to student support and more institutional flexibility. The majority of our participants believe that, were they to return to study, they could operationalise the knowledge gained through 'dropping out'. Rather than being serial 'failures', they would thus be well equipped to make the most of the university opportunity.

4 The impacts of working-class 'drop out'

Introduction

In this chapter, we draw on the interview data, plus data from the research jury days to analyse the impacts of early withdrawal, not just on students themselves, but also on the universities and the areas where they are located.

Impacts on student identity

While retention research and institutional strategies to improve retention rates are clearly important, our findings challenge the current emphasis on institutions to retain students at all costs. Such an emphasis equates retention (or completion) with success and, consequently, non-completion with failure. Although 'drop out' can be traumatic, many students do not regard their decision to leave early as negative. On the contrary, they gain positive experiences from having attended university, if only for a very short time, and this can help them to move forward with their lives.

The decision to withdraw early is a very personal one and inevitably the implications are felt most strongly by the individual concerned. Not surprisingly, the way students reflect on their decision to leave early differs according to their reasons for leaving early and their experience of the process of leaving (e.g. the level of support given). For example, one student was forced to withdraw after only four days because the subjects she wanted to study were not available. Consequently, she was very critical of the institution involved and had lodged a formal complaint. She received no support from the university and had to approach them herself some weeks later to see if she could defer for a year. She described being initially 'absolutely devastated' but, during her year out, has found a good job (which she will be able to continue part-time when she restarts at university) and has obtained an additional A-level qualification:

> The only thing I can say that this year has done to me is that it's given me a bit of independence and confidence. Before I was one of those people who didn't use to talk to many people. Now I'm really open, I have a lot of avenues. I'm quite happy now about going to university.
> (Female)

Students experience mixed emotions following their withdrawal – a sense of both relief and regret:

> In a sense I feel I have let myself down. In another I feel I have been a bit brave in deciding it wasn't for me and that I wanted to do something else and not waste time.
> (Female)

> I was upset because I didn't finish the course. I did feel a bit of a failure really because I didn't actually complete it. On the other hand, because it was running me down, I did feel relief because I was just physically low. I did feel more relaxed when I left, but I did feel upset that I didn't finish. If I had finished I would have been flying.
> (Female)

Even when individuals are confident they have made the right decision they often feel a sense of disappointment that they started something they did not complete. For example, one female student had been forced to leave early because of external commitments (i.e. work and children). Although she was very happy with the course, the arrival of her baby meant that there were just too many other demands on her time:

> I was very disappointed in myself but I had to be realistic about what was going on. I had to wake up and smell the coffee. It was running me down – not the course itself, but all the aspects of what was going on. As far as people being surprised about me finishing, I think because they could see there was a lot for me to do I don't think they were too surprised. They could see that something had to go. They were not unsupportive towards me. If there was anything that anybody could have done, they would have done it. They didn't pressurise me in any way; the main choice was completely up to me. I didn't have any hassle from them for making the choice that I did.
> (Female)

Students' confidence can take a significant knock if they leave early, irrespective of the reason behind their withdrawal. For example, one student who left because she was dissatisfied with the course, as it was not what she had expected or wanted to pursue, still felt that leaving had caused her to question her own abilities:

> I couldn't figure out whether or not it was me. Perhaps I couldn't handle the work or was it the fact that I got so bored that I didn't want to handle

the work and I let it slip. I couldn't figure either of them out really. So yes my confidence did take a bit of a knock.
(Female)

For some students the depth of these feelings was evident. The following comment was made by a student who was extremely unhappy at university to the extent that she became ill with worry, but still felt that leaving had been damaging for her:

> I am not a person who leaves things. I can't come this far just to chuck it away. I am not that kind of person. I was heartbroken. I was really sad and I thought it was the end of my life.
> (Female)

The way students feel about their decision is also affected by the perceptions and reactions of others, such as friends, family and employers. Some students felt they were letting not only themselves but also others down by leaving early. Many students felt that, while their parents did not initially want them to leave, ultimately they just wanted them to 'be happy':

How individuals perceive their decision to withdraw early changes over time. Clearly, perceptions were affected by post-university experiences, for example what employment they had been able to obtain or what other opportunities they saw as available to them. The extent to which ex-students were in contact with other students who were able to successfully complete their degrees also affected perceptions of their own experience. Many students were not immediately able to feel positive about their decision, but with time this altered. Others were initially relieved to be out of university but with time they questioned their decision:

> When I left I thought perhaps I ought to have stayed. Maybe. But given time now I feel I have done the right thing. Now I can just move on and do what I need to do.
> (Female)

> I was relieved. I had it niggling away at me that I didn't want to be there. Looking back now, I don't know if I regret it. One of the boys who was doing the same course as me; lives in the same street as me; we have been friends all our lives, he is in his last year now. I do think sometimes, if I'd only stuck at it.
> (Female)

> I didn't feel like a failure ... the job I am doing now is directly related to the course I was doing. If I wasn't doing this job I would feel a bit worthless. I would feel I hadn't achieved anything. I got the promotion because of my coursework. I feel that I achieved something from it. (Male)

Length of attendance at university is important. A student who has completed only a few weeks before leaving is likely to feel differently to someone who withdraws after two years. Similarly, some students left with a form of qualification whereas others received nothing and so perceived their experience as a complete waste of time.

Michael's story

Michael comes from a working-class background and is an only child. His parents always told him that education was important and he enjoyed school where he was pushed to work hard and encouraged to go on to university. Michael feels that people in his community have positive attitudes towards higher education – they know it is the way forward. Most of the people in Michael's class were going on to university so he decided to go also. He didn't want to move too far away from his home town, as his parents and friends are important to him so, when he was offered a place, he took it:

> Initially, I wanted to do HND in computing. I looked at the degree course and I thought it would be too difficult for me ... When I first spoke to the university they told me the HND course was running, when I came to sign they announced that this course is no longer available. They then told me about this computer science course. I had only put one option on my UCAS, so then I panicked because I had everything set up for going. I had halls to stay in. I panicked – everyone else was going. I didn't want to be left at home when everybody else was away. I knew it was an opportunity to get more education and I decided to go for it. Looking back at it now, it definitely was too much. An HND would have been much better. When the university told me that it wouldn't be available I should have looked for other options instead. I just panicked and did the degree.

> The class sizes were very big. There was no personal contact ... I enjoy studying but there was no personal contact when I got into problems with the course. It was very intimidating, sitting in a class of 150. The lecturer didn't even know you. If I had a problem it was difficult to get some help, then that problem would get worse and worse ... It would have been better

Continued

> if they'd taught us in small groups where we could sit down at the PC and show us what they meant instead of just talking and talking … There were times when I found it really hard to cope with.

Michael did seek help but was not offered any advice about changing course:

> It was a case of, it is your course, you picked it, and you are in it … If I could have changed to another subject that had similar modules maybe I could have changed instead of dropping out and wasting the year, leaving with nothing … I stayed until May … more or less to the exams. I realised that in no way was I fit to do them. The course was too much.

Michael would have liked some advice when he told the university that he was dropping out, but wasn't given any. He is now doing an HND in business IT at college. Asked what he would have done differently if he could wind the clock back, Michael said he would definitely go to university to study business IT because it would be more suited to him.

Students highlighted a number of wider benefits they felt they had gained from their university experience, such as a sense of regaining control and independent decision making, valuable life experience, improved communication skills and increased self-confidence:

> I know I can make my own decisions. I was always a bit dubious about that. Now I know I can do things for myself.
> (Male)

> I got a life experience out of it. I was sitting in a classroom with a wide range of people around me, aged from 16 to 45. It was amazing.
> (Female)

> … at interview I had more to talk about when they asked questions about how I worked as part of a team, how I communicated effectively, how I communicated with others. Had I not gone to university at all I think it would have made it much more difficult for me.
> (Male)

> It's made me confident. I'm happy with what I'm doing now … it has helped me. I know what I want to do now.
> (Male)

For many students, the process had been one of self-discovery. They had developed a clearer idea of what they wanted to do in the future; what they liked and disliked in terms of subject, teaching methods and assessment, etc.; what they were good at in terms of preferred learning styles:

> I feel a bit surer now of where I want to go with my life in general. I'm still not 100 per cent there but I am a bit more confident of where I am going in terms of a career.
> (Female)

> I am more confident in my work. I am enjoying it. I think I am more of a working person than a learning person.
> (Female)

> I wouldn't look at it as positive or negative. I just look at it as a learning curve. I tried it and it wasn't for me.
> (Male)

> I suppose it gave me the chance to see what I really wanted to do, and what I didn't want to do.
> (Female)

Impacts on employment opportunities

The destinations of those who had withdrawn early were varied and seemed to indicate that, with some exceptions, going to university and withdrawing early had not helped their employment prospects. Twelve of the participants had already returned to study. Only eight had found management positions or joined professions such as the police force. The majority of positions taken up by the remainder were unskilled or semi-skilled in nature. Ten of the participants found themselves unemployed (see Figure 2):

> I am working at the moment. I am a care assistant with homeless people, working in a homeless hostel. It is something I have wanted to do for a while but I've never really got round to it.
> (Female)

> I work in Somerfields, checkouts, shelf stacking, all the basic rubbish stuff.
> (Female)

Figure 2 Current status of participants by institution

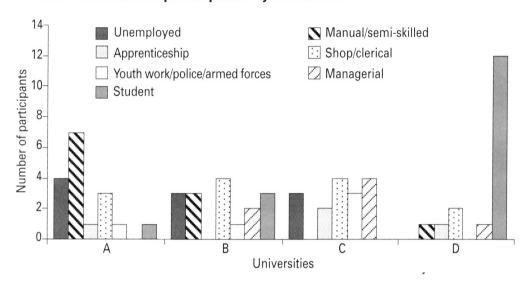

Although many students were able to react in a positive manner to leaving early, they did not believe employers shared this attitude. They sensed some stigma to being a student who did not complete their course and so had decided to omit this from their CV, offering further information about leaving early only if directly questioned:

> If I told them I went to university and got asked what qualifications did I get, and I replied I didn't get any, it would give the impression that I'm not up for the job.
> (Male)

> I did mention it but I only mentioned that I only did the one year. It's still embarrassing for me.
> (Female)

For students working part time while at university, this strategy had been facilitated by their employment and this was frequently used to 'cover up' their attendance and subsequent withdrawal:

> I will probably hide it away. I was still working at ASDA during that time so that can be hidden away.
> (Female)

Others felt it important to include their university experience on future applications to courses and/or employment:

> I wrote down everything when I applied. They asked why I'd left. I
> explained that obviously it wasn't for me and I just didn't feel that I was
> meeting every achievement I wanted to. They were fine really.
> (Male)

> I think it goes for you. Even though I didn't complete it, it still shows
> initiative that I actually went to university. When people ask me why I left I
> tell my situation.
> (Male)

Some students simply ceased attendance at university and converted their existing
part-time employment to a full-time position:

> I was still working at the sports shop part time when I left. When I left
> university I asked for more hours and got them more or less straight
> away. I ended up full time.
> (Female)

Other students experienced difficulty finding employment once they had left
university:

> It hasn't stopped me going for every job I can apply for. I just haven't got
> anywhere. I've applied for over 40 jobs and when I get a reply they just
> say I don't meet their requirements.
> (Male)

In contrast, a further group used their university experience to their advantage. For
example, one participant was a computer studies student who fell behind in his
coursework because of the time spent in part-time employment. Having completed
two years, he left and was employed as a manual labourer in a warehouse. The
company's personnel department, however, noted his university experience and he
subsequently moved into the IT department, eventually taking up a management
position.

Following the decision to leave university early, employment opportunities and
pathways are related to the way the early leaver views themselves within the context
of non-completion. For a number of students, making the decision to leave was a
boost to their self-confidence and their self-realisation. Where leaving early was
taken as an opportunity to exercise independent decision-making skills, this
appeared to enhance employability:

> I went for a job at the Inland Revenue. I applied and went through four or five different tests and interview stages. Four and a half thousand people had applied. I was one of four successful applicants. That boosted my self-confidence. I am actually doing very well.
> (Male)

However, where the withdrawal is framed in negativity, employability may be proportionally affected.

A number of students felt that a suitable compromise between full-time study and part-time employment was to reverse the situation and become a part-time student in full-time employment. However, very few students were offered the option of changing from full-time to part-time study. Where a student did wish to continue studying, the common option they were given was to either repeat a year or rejoin a course after a year out:

> She said that if I wanted to just put my course on hold I could either finish the year and take a year out and go back and start the second year, or I could go on hold now and start again in September.
> (Female)

Impacts on attitudes to education

Perhaps the most positive indication of the leaving-early experience is the students' desire to ultimately return to education. Of all the students interviewed, 20 had either already returned to higher education or seriously intended to do so in the near future:

Researcher:	Would you recommend going to university to other people?
Interviewee (male):	I would recommend it but I would only recommend it to the ones who know they want to go. I would not push anyone into it. If they want to go I would give them advice. It isn't for everyone. People need to know what they want to do and what they want to get out of it. Not just jump in.

Many others envisaged a university education as playing a role in their future. Only one said they would never want to return to university again. The view that students who 'drop out' are permanently 'lost' to education is not supported by this research.

The significant change was that they now viewed education in a more strategic way as a means to an end that they needed to define more clearly for themselves:

> *Researcher:*   Just to sort of ask you again, it hasn't put you off learning?
>
> *Interviewee (male):*   No, it has just pointed out what I should have been doing in the first place. When I do finish my apprenticeship it does give me an HND, which is obviously lower than a degree, so it hasn't put me off trying maybe later on to continue for another year to get a degree, so it hasn't put me off education at all.

One could argue that they had moved from being passive to active in redefining their goals and that 'drop out' can be understood as the first stage in that process:

> It has just made me wake up and think about what I want.
> (Male)

That end might be vocational but there were also discourses of pleasure in learning. They also wanted to take advantage of any flexibility that did exist in the system that they had previously not known about:

> Even though I didn't finish I think it was still a worthwhile experience and I think it still set me up and prepared me for life. I didn't feel any shame.
> (Female)

Peter's story

Peter comes from a working-class background and was the first in his family to go to university. His family's attitude is that they would support him whatever he chose to do. The vast majority of his friends are students. Peter knew that he wanted to be a policeman and the school's career adviser suggested doing a university course in social science prior to seeking to join the police. He signed up, attending as a day student, and stayed between two and three months before realising it wasn't for him:

Continued

> To be perfectly honest, I think it was as much my fault as anybody giving me advice. Looking back now I should have certainly looked into the course and seen what was there ... I was a bit gullible ... When I got there I didn't really know what was involved in the course, sociology and psychology and things like that, which I wasn't really too interested in.

Peter realised that he was not enjoying the course and started speaking to police officers who told him that he could get into the police force via another route. He hadn't at this stage made contact with any individual tutors so he went to the administration staff and told them he was dropping out. They told him to send a letter to them about his withdrawal, but didn't suggest he talk to anyone before taking the final decision:

> With hindsight and looking back, it was a bit strange that they thought 'why has he picked this course and thrown in the towel already?' I thought, looking back, someone might have wanted to discuss it with me.

Peter summed up his experiences:

> A combination of bad advice and my naivety just to dive straight in with someone else's advice.

Impacts on institutions

'Drop out' is currently constructed as a failure of both student and institution. Funding arrangements ensure that institutions are heavily penalised for 'drop out'. In effect, they are sanctioned rather than rewarded for attempting to widen participation. High drop-out rates potentially threaten the very survival of the institutions involved:

> What are the consequences of 'drop out'? Well clearly a big one is the university's prospects. If we don't keep them there will be financial implications.
> (Head of recruitment)

'Drop out' and the way in which it was handled was seen as having a long-term impact on the university's future ambitions and missions, and on its credibility within the local community:

> The university's mission is to become very much a local university resource for the local population ... that means the students of today, if

> we've already got over 50 per cent of our students from the local area,
> are going to be the parents of the students of tomorrow … if withdrawal is
> done in a supportive, kind, safe, well-meaning environment, then, when
> they're advising their own children about coming here or not, that's likely
> to have left a positive impression.
> (Lecturer)

Impacts on localities

This research has positioned the universities as an integral part of their local
communities. One of the purposes of the jury days was to explore the perceived
impact of 'drop out' on these already disadvantaged locales. It is difficult to quantify
impacts of 'drop out' but some shared effects were suggested and traced.

High rates of working-class withdrawal had an impact on local morale. 'Drop out' was
seen as having a 'knock-on effect' on the local community and as spreading
disillusionment to networks of families and friends:

> It spreads disaffection across the community in small pockets.
> (Adviser, student services)

It added to a climate of confusion where students and their families have lost the old
certainties of traditional industries and are caught between the pull to employment,
the lack of real job opportunities and the supposed promises of education:

> I live on a council estate … people from that kind of place think that
> education isn't important and you're getting that drummed into you all the
> time, that you don't need to get an education, get a job, go into an
> industry but industry is very low now in this area. The effect of 'drop out'
> on the community is morale as well … they hear you saying 'oh I couldn't
> manage it at university' and they think, 'oh maybe I shouldn't go either'.
> (Participant facilitator/student who had dropped out)

This chain of disappointment could be perpetuated once students try to re-enter the
labour market:

> If they match them to the wrong job they come back and they're even
> more down and even more disadvantaged.
> (Adviser, Job Centre Plus)

'Drop out' impacted on the public image of the area and tended to perpetuate an already negative perception of the place and its occupants as unsuccessful:

> I think it's part of a perception of a failing area with things like being
> labelled the worst city.
> (President, Students' Union)

'Drop out' affected the motivation of potential students and was seen as disproportionately impacting on working-class students. Middle-class students were already cushioned and on track, whereas 'drop out' counteracted all the efforts to 'raise aspirations' in working-class communities:

> There's a well-trodden path from a lot of schools sector into higher
> education. That can be seen almost as apathy … I think likewise there's
> this brick wall that has to be dismantled in terms of some of the other
> areas. If we don't do something to improve or reduce the drop-out rates
> looking at the human cost of all the mismatching, then it does filter down,
> right down into the community where we're actually trying to influence
> people to come through. It does reinforce those images of university as
> elitist. It costs too much to go to university. It's too hard to go to university.
> I couldn't possibly do the course … I think it's a bit of an indictment that
> we're maybe failing to recognise and cope with those early signs of
> potential dropout.
> (Head of recruitment)

'Drop out' was even seen as hindering young people from being active citizens, for example acting as a barrier to participating in the voluntary sector:

> I sit on recruitment panels for local charities and up until today I would
> have disregarded people who had dropped out for appointments in the
> voluntary sector.
> (Participant, research jury day)

Impacts on regeneration

The Government is asking universities to play an important role in regeneration. Moreover, local partnerships with other educational institutions, the public sector and industry are seen as key to the future developments of all the institutions in our study. However, 'drop out' was seen as a counteracting force:

> One of the consequences of 'drop out' for us is that we have lots of unfilled posts and in some cases we aren't able to meet our statutory obligations. We're unable to plan for the future or give best value to the community and projects are delayed and people's needs not identified.
> (Local authority representative, research jury day)

Universities were charged with improving the local skills base but 'drop out' was perceived as a threat to that process:

> It's very much dependent on technical skills to really support the knowledge-based economy. We've also got very much an SME-based economy and it's dependent on entrepreneurial thinkers with the proper skills to set up things like this in the future. So I think that's really the impact of 'drop out' on the region.
> (Computer science lecturer)

Ultimately, 'drop out' impacted on the future economic growth of the region:

> The consequences of 'drop out' for the area are quite simple. It's a deprived area round here. It is below the EU-stated poverty line. Without students going to university I don't think it's going to be able to get out of that. It's a Catch-22 situation: you need the students to go to university in order to increase the economic standing of the area. Not many big businesses want to come to an area where the population isn't educated … like I say it goes round and round.
> (Education officer, Students' Union)

Conclusion

We have seen that the reasons for 'drop out' are complex and multiple, and so too with the impacts of 'drop out'. Withdrawing early, although it can be traumatic, can have positive consequences in helping students to redefine their priorities and their directions. They are also able to utilise the skills and life experiences they have gained from their stay in university, making it more than just a waste of time. However, the way that 'drop out' is dominantly constructed mitigates against those positive learning outcomes that students have gained from their experience at university and that we have outlined in this chapter. It is generally, although not always, a disadvantage in the labour market. It also produces very negative consequences for institutions and localities. Our research has revealed the importance of cross-sectoral collaboration and dialogue in unpeeling some of these layers and addressing early withdrawal and its negative impacts:

> The worlds of education are all parcelled up. How do we help students and our own staff make connections and transitions? We need progression through transparency.
> (Chair, research jury day)

However, we would go further and argue for structural change, rather than just greater clarity within the existing system. We believe that the answer to the 'problem' of working-class 'drop out' is to reframe lifelong learning, drawing on knowledge from other countries.

5 Reframing lifelong learning and student 'drop out'

In this chapter, we draw on the findings of the international colloquium and the international research reports. We also use data from interviews with university careers and employment services, and from a survey of those involved in admissions, plus further data from the student interviews and research jury days.

Introduction

Our research with young working-class students who have withdrawn from higher education found that many students were 'captured' by the dominant view that this experience should be perceived as a 'disaster' and that the young people concerned are 'failures':

> I was worried about being seen as a disappointment, or some sort of failure.
> (Female)

But the in-depth nature of this research was able to reveal more about the decisions made, the feelings involved and the subsequent consequences. These findings undermine the dominant discourse of failure associated with leaving early. This chapter of the report focuses on this challenge, and traces the implications and possibilities for reframing lifelong learning and student withdrawal. It draws on data from the student interviews, research jury days, and the international colloquium and policy seminar, interviews with university careers and employment services, and the admissions survey.

Young people

The majority of young people took the decisions carefully and thoughtfully:

> I didn't find it an easy decision. I took lots of things into consideration. I didn't want to stay just for my friends. I wanted to do what was right for myself.
> (Female)

Either at the time or on reflection, the students tended to feel that leaving was the correct decision, and that making this tough decision had had benefits for them:

> It just made me realise that there are other areas to be explored. For me, leaving was a positive experience.
> (Male)

Students gained from their decision in a number of ways.

■ An *informed decision* about entering/not entering higher education based on experience: this is likely to be of greater significance to students who are the first in their family to attend university and so do not have access to 'hot knowledge.'

■ Increased *knowledge about specific disciplines* and awareness of the subject area they do/do not want to study: many of the students in the study had made decisions about which course to study based on very limited information. Some left with the intention of re-entering a different discipline area in the future.

■ Greater *confidence* having tried higher education and made a decision to leave (which can be contrasted with a non-decision to enter HE): this gave some students confidence in their own ability to make decisions and to pursue their own pathways.

■ *Opportunities* to pursue alternative pathways, which included entering directly into employment and careers, changing courses or institutions and reorienting the direction of their lives: some students had felt that few alternative opportunities were available to them as they were making their post-18 transition.

These 'benefits', as the students perceive them, indicate that leaving early should not necessarily be termed in wholly negative terms. The negative implications of early withdrawal for students, institutions and the local area are not intrinsic, but are created by higher education policy and cultural norms.

Structural and attitudinal factors contribute to students' feelings of failure, institutions being labelled as 'failing' and being penalised financially too, and the local society and economy not benefiting from the skills of these ex-students as fully as they might do.

Student withdrawal within a lifelong learning context

Examination of current norms and policies reveals that the higher education system in the UK is still premised on traditional and elite conceptions about the nature of HE students and the appropriate type of provision. Policy makers focus their widening participation targets on those under 30. Students are largely assumed to be young (entering directly or almost immediately from school or college), studying full-time, with family financial support and little or no outside responsibilities or concerns. They are normally expected to study for a three- or four-year honours degree, based at the HEI, and to live on the campus or nearby.

The crucial assumption underpinning this view of higher education is that students *can* and *should* complete their higher education in three (or four years) with no interruptions. Any deviation from this model is perceived to be a reflection of either student or institutional failure. This motif of failure is continued into the labour market: students who leave higher education without achieving their target qualification are given less support in securing appropriate employment than their peers who have either graduated or not entered HE; and employers can be reluctant to recognise the skills that people have gained from their period in higher education.

An alternative model of higher education would abandon these assumptions and associated prejudices, which effectively discriminate against non-traditional students and those from under-represented groups. Key features of a higher education system that supports lifelong learning would include the following.

■ Actively counteracts long-term and intergenerational cumulative disadvantages and does not imply individual or institutional culpability as the norm.

■ Wide range of sites of higher education, with parity and complete transferability between them.

■ Multiple entry and exit points – and promotes moving in and out of HE as both positive and 'normal'.

■ Flexible entry requirements.

■ Abandoning the false full- and part-time distinction, and offering all courses in different modes.

■ Support for students to enter and exit at different points. This may include personal planning of a route through higher education, and careers support to enter the labour market and institutional support to change courses, mode of study, etc.

■ Wide range of exit opportunities (including, but not restricted to, qualifications).

■ Effective credit accumulation and transfer scheme within and between HEIs.

■ Tracking of students' progress and transition into and out of education and employment.

■ No restrictive assumptions about the duration of study (this may include 'fast-track' routes as well as longer completion times) and longer time lapses before students are deemed to have withdrawn.

■ An effective and fair extenuating circumstances system that recognises the additional pressures and commitments some students face.

■ Comprehensive provision of childcare and other services to support students with more complicated personal lives 'round the clock'.

■ No financial penalties for institutions or students who take different routes through HE, perhaps through a voucher system or similar.

■ Fees payable for units studied, rather than number of years of registration.

■ A commitment to maintain the breadth of the curriculum and expansion as necessary.

■ Improved learning, teaching and assessment to support a more diverse and dynamic student body.

■ Actively following up and encouraging people who have exited at all points to re-enter at a wide range of levels.

■ Transparent policy for students at all stages and staff, in particular admissions officers, personal tutors and guidance and support staff.

The current UK climate makes the need for an HE system that promotes lifelong learning more urgent. Key issues include economic change, skill shortages and the introduction of new qualifications, a commitment to widening participation and the introduction of top-up fees in England.

The UK labour market has undergone significant change in the last 25 to 30 years. It is widely argued that the majority of the population can no longer anticipate working in the same job or even employment sector throughout their career. Furthermore, it is predicted that people will need to work for longer (for example, to the age of 65 or 70). People will therefore need to move in and out of education and training, including HE.

Labour market analysis demonstrates that there is a shortage of intermediate skills in the UK. This was reinforced by some employers in the research jury days. In Scotland, for example, skills such as languages were emphasised and, in Northern Ireland, computing was highlighted. Employers therefore need to be supported and encouraged to employ students during their studies, after part-completion of an honours degree and with alternative higher education qualifications (HE certificates and diplomas, Higher National certificates and diplomas, foundation degrees and other level 4 qualifications).

The 2004 Higher Education Act introduced foundation degrees (FDs) in England. FDs are premised on work-based learning, and therefore the majority of students will be in work, older, part-time and studying away from the main HEI site. These students may therefore need the flexibility and support identified above.

The 2004 Higher Education Act also introduced top-up fees and reinforced the Government's commitment to widening participation. In England, this combination is likely to result in more first-generation entrants from lower-income groups entering higher education, under greater financial strain. This study demonstrates the need for a more flexible model of higher education to support young working-class students to succeed. Government policies may result in students entering HE at a later age and combining studying with larger amounts of paid work and other commitments.

International evidence and perspectives

This section of the report draws on international evidence presented at the research colloquium. Our UK-based study has sought to draw on international evidence and perspectives to explore the meanings and implications of young working-class 'drop out'. This is particularly helpful in relation to reframing lifelong learning and student 'drop out'. The need for a reformed structure of higher education, which is more suitable to meet the needs of greater student diversity and a post-industrial economy, is demonstrated in the international context:

> Dropping out is only the last link of a whole chain of selection processes blocking their *[students from lower socio-economic groups]* path to a university degree.
> (Heublein, 2004, p. 1)

The German education system is structured in such a way that social, cultural and economic disadvantages are not compensated for during early education, and thus these disadvantages are perpetuated and reinforced throughout the educational system. Similarly, in Ireland, students from lower socio-economic groups are less likely to complete secondary education, they tend to achieve lower grades and even with the requisite grades they are less likely to transfer to HE (Carpenter, 2004). Research in Australia demonstrates that students may be members of more than one group that is under-represented in higher education and issues may compound each other, producing extreme disadvantage (Heagney, 2004, p. 5). In the UK, there is a long history of primary and secondary education seeking to overcome social, cultural and economic disadvantages, but these, at best, have only ever had a limited effect. Thus, in the UK, working-class students have negative learning trajectories too; broad social reform is required, but, as part of the process, the higher education sector needs to be transformed to better accommodate the needs of these students. This includes offering students flexible multiple-entry and exit points and the associated support to top up their education throughout their lives.

Heagney, talking from an Australian perspective, raises the difficulty of the terminology used for 'drop out':

> Are we talking about retention, attrition, non-completion, intra or inter-institutional transfer or 'drop out'?
> (Heagney, 2004, p. 1)

Australian research studies have found that many students who 'drop out' return to study later on:

> This suggests that dropping out cannot always be equated with failure.
> (Heagney, 2004, p. 12)

Indeed, if withdrawal is, at least in part, a consequence of cumulative disadvantage, framing it in such negative terms is inappropriate and counterproductive:

> Successful drop outs have been described as those who get the job they want or those who withdraw temporarily or permanently from their

> studies, but who are eligible to continue studies at that university. Others
> whose dropping out could be considered successful are those who leave
> for personal reasons (family or financial) before they have completed
> their course, but for whom university has been demystified.
> (Heagney 2004, p. 12)

In the UK, a student is deemed to have withdrawn from higher education after a comparatively short period (determined initially by internal institutional mechanisms and reinforced by annual reporting structures to HESA). In Canada, a much longer time frame is employed:

> To be classified as having dropped out, a student must be absent for
> more than six consecutive semesters.
> (Bonin, 2004, p. 4)

In European countries such as Germany, longer periods of non-studying are allowed too. This enables students to extend the duration of their studying to accommodate personal circumstances, financial and employment issues, and slower rates of studying.

In keeping with the findings in this study, Australian research demonstrates that:

> Students are much more vulnerable to dropping out if they are
> dissatisfied with the course they have chosen.
> (Heagney, 2004, p. 10)

For some students, wrong course choice results in deferment; for others, this choice does not exist. It is therefore crucial that students are supported and facilitated to change course.

Changing mode of study also needs to be facilitated. Some students interviewed in this research had not considered reducing their study load, which would have either eased the academic burden or provided an opportunity to earn and learn, and thus supported completion. In Australia, the distinction between full-time and part-time study is becoming increasingly blurred. This needs to be formalised in the UK in recognition of the need of the majority of students to engage in employment.

In most countries in our study, poor student finance contributes to higher rates of withdrawal among students from lower socio-economic groups. In a German study:

> Almost a third of the student drop-outs from working-class families cited difficulties in funding their studies as the decisive reason for prematurely leaving university. This proportion is only half as high in other groups.
> (Heublein, 2004, p. 7)

Adequate funding for students from lower socio-economic groups would therefore go a long way towards improving student retention. In addition, students who do change course or institution, or who need to work, should not be further penalised – the system should accommodate their needs. Financial support linked to academic achievement is punitive for both individuals and institutions.

A consequence of a more inclusive, lifelong learning model of higher education would be the participation of older students, who are more likely to have family responsibilities. In Germany, working-class students tend to be older than their peers, as they have not come through the grammar school route, but through 'second-chance' and vocational routes. Incompatibility between family commitments and course obligations contributes to the early withdrawal of these students (Heublein, 2004, p. 9). This problem could be exacerbated in the UK by a lifelong learning model of HE unless adequate support and understanding is available.

In addition, a lifelong learning model of HE would need to be supported by facilities such as credit accumulation and transfer, and effective tracking to facilitate this process. Heagney notes:

> … although students move in and out of higher education and employment, very little tracking of these movements takes place.
> (Heagney, 2004, p. 11)

Contributions from Australia, Ireland and Germany all noted a cultural mismatch between what is offered by higher education and the expectations of students from lower socio-economic groups – this includes pedagogies, values, knowledge systems and curricula contents. German research shows that this is particularly pronounced in subject areas:

> … strongly characterised by social selectivity that is medicine and law.
> (Heublein, 2004, p. 8)

Similarly, in Ireland:

> Cultural discontinuities were also experienced by working-class students
> within higher education as they felt their class backgrounds were neither
> reflected nor affirmed within colleges.
> (Lynch, 1999, p. 123)

The major changes in Croatia since independence from the former Yugoslavia have
presented opportunities unparalleled in any of the other countries studied to
restructure their higher education system:

> The Strategy of Development of the Republic of Croatia for the 21st
> Century highlights the importance of youth and adult education, and the
> need for informal education and self-education. This government strategy
> puts an accent on two concepts ... the concepts of lifelong learning and a
> learning society.
> (Vladacek-Hains *et al.*, 2004, p. 6)

The UK must create an opportunity to transform the existing higher education system
into one that promotes and facilitates lifelong learning for all its citizens, otherwise it
risks being left behind by the knowledge economy.

Comparing and contrasting current UK approaches with a lifelong learning model of higher education

This section of the report considers the current strengths and weaknesses of the
participating UK HEIs in supporting a lifelong learning model of higher education. It
uses data from interviews and responses to structured questions with admissions
tutors, careers service personnel and agencies supporting students to find (part-
time) employment.

The focus of admissions processes tends to be on fair decision making and
transparency, rather than seeking to counteract earlier disadvantage. The impact of
the Schwartz (2004) report remains to be seen, but it may well be interpreted as
promoting the former rather than the latter. Some universities, however, do appear to
be more flexible, considering the ability of the student to succeed and the other skills
that an applicant possesses, rather than qualifications. This approach ought to be
developed and promoted.

The distinction between full- and part-time modes of studying remains rigid. In each institution, students can change but this has to be agreed on a one-to-one basis, and there can be difficulties when part-time courses do not exist:

> Where possible a study regime can be agreed to facilitate special personal circumstances. This is obviously made easier where a part-time version of the course already exists.
> (Admissions officer)

This process is supported by a specialist student guidance officer in one institution and a large part-time programme in another:

> We've got a big part-time programme and students can come back part-time and a lot of them do actually come back.
> (Careers adviser)

There is no evidence of seamless movement between modes of study, or of students being in control of the number of modules they want to study. Studying part-time also has financial implications, with students unable to access the forms of financial support available to those who are full-time.

Changing course is largely viewed as problematic because of limited numbers of places and a potential mismatch between what has been studied to date and future course requirements. The student guidance officer in one institution can ameliorate this. There is potential for this role to be expanded into personal planning of HE pathways.

Institutions have different views about supporting students to switch to another HEI. One admissions officer commented:

> We would try our best to hold onto any student unless they were determined to get out.

While an officer in another institution said:

> No problem, better to find a suitable course.

And a third university assisted their students with this process:

> The student guidance officer *[SGO]* can advise the student on how to go about transferring. The SGO will also advise the student to visit the careers department for information on the new institution.

Although each institution has a process for intermitting, readmitting students was implicitly viewed as difficult. There were references to courses changing, knowledge going out of date and study skills declining. The concept of multiple exit and (re) entry points has a long way to go.

Admissions staff were broadly supportive of accrediting the achievements of exiting students, but this was not widely implemented. Guidance staff were supportive, but hazy about the details:

> Oh yes. Say you've somebody who's already completed their first year and then they can already claim for a certificate can't they?
> (Careers adviser)

The emphasis is on students seeking the credit if they want it, rather than a more proactive model on the part of the universities.

There is good advice and support available for students either changing their mode of study or course, or withdrawing. But it is not taken up by many students:

> Too many students just drift off/disappear without discussing it with a member of staff. At the end of the year we have to withdraw students because they just have not told us they are leaving.

When students are thinking about leaving they do not appear to be directed to or take advantage of the advice available to them to enter the labour market and use the skills (and qualifications) they have gained from higher education:

> It would be helpful when a student first says they're thinking of dropping out of the course if they were advised to come to the careers service. I think that would be a major step.
> (Careers service)

Data collected in this study found that university staff are very wary about promoting support available to students who want to change or withdraw:

> We felt that to talk about dropping out at induction would give a negative impression.
> (Careers adviser)

Not talking about exiting and re-entering HE reinforces the idea that movement and change are not the norm and that they are problematic. It is also counter-intuitive for students who know well that early withdrawal is commonplace. A lifelong learning model of higher education would require institutions to talk about routes into and out of education and employment, and provide support for them. Institutions are providing information about leaving and the need to work with the careers service in a variety of ways:

- post-induction careers activities

- personal tutor referrals: this requires awareness raising among tutors

- leaflets:

   We have leaflets printed for people who are thinking of discontinuing and to guide them through the thought processes that they need to go through. It emphasises things like not making a hasty decision and not assuming that the course really isn't for them when all they need is to give it a chance and settle down.
   (Admissions)

Students who are withdrawing often visit university services with a sense of finality and failure:

   Feelings of panic and disappointment, great concern about what's going to happen … Sometimes feelings of negativity, failure, that sort of thing happens as well. Sometimes a person has made the decision and is just coming along to do the formalities and they're perfectly OK about it.
   (Careers adviser)

But, in some ways, the support offered is similar, based on a model of the needs of the individual:

   If you're a graduate, it's like – I've come to the end of the road; I have to make a decision about what I have to do, which is sometimes a great shock to people. In some ways people who are leaving early face the same dilemmas, it's just the road came to an end perhaps earlier than they planned.
   (Careers adviser)

Similar strategies can be employed:

   It's finding a way, career planning and career management just as graduates would do as well.
   (Careers adviser)

In terms of progression routes for graduates and those leaving early there can be a significant difference; this is largely dependent on the level at which students exit. Some university careers services felt that they were not the best people to advise these students because:

> We don't have the kind of vacancies that they would be going for.
> (Careers adviser)

Others saw it differently:

> Say two years experience of HE, there are quite a few graduate options they can still go into.

Careers advisers have had little or no training in this area.

Universities and colleges increasingly have 'job shops' or other services to support students to secure appropriate part-time employment. These services offer a potential mechanism to strengthen routes into and out of higher education, but they do not currently see their role in this way, although each service identified full-time jobs that might be suitable for intermitting or withdrawing students.

Such an approach would have benefits for both students and institutions. Students would have an opportunity to develop work-related skills that would assist them in the short and long term. They would also have the opportunity to try working in a particular field or sector, which could inform their study choices. Periods of full-time employment, followed by full-time (or even fast-track) studying may be more efficient than trying to combine working and studying. For HEIs, a relationship would be established between themselves and the exiting student and potentially the employer:

> There are added benefits. It ties a person into the university, particularly in the instance where somebody finishes in November because they did the wrong course but they will reapply for something else the following September. But, by working for the *[student employment agency]* on a full-time basis, we could tie somebody in *[to the university]*.
> (Student employment agency)

For such a mechanism to add value to a high street recruitment agency, their role would need to be explicit:

> The only thing we would have to change from our side is the accessibility in making sure people are aware that we were an option. That people could fairly easily work in a full-time environment that was going to link them in with the university still.

This could be achieved in part by:

> Linking ourselves up with the student support side who have people who have dropped out, it would give them an additional string to the bow to get full-time employment if they needed it.
> (Student employment agency)

When it comes to re-entering the labour market, it seems that students who have withdrawn early are not well served. Representatives from Job Centre Plus who took part in the research jury days saw themselves as catering mainly for the unskilled or semi-skilled unemployed. They receive no training and have little experience in advising students who have dropped out to re-engage with the full-time labour market. Indeed, when Job Centres were approached at a later stage to take part in more detailed interviews, three out of four declined, arguing that this client group was not within their remit. This is a structural issue with repercussions for staff development. This problem is further reinforced by operational practices: rigid benefit restrictions compound the problems of 'drop out' by perpetuating poverty and relegating students who 'drop out' to a lesser employment market:

> They see no worth in themselves and we're just given half-an-hour interview to tackle this. They're disenchanted and bitter and are also unrealistic in their expectations. Because they haven't got a recognised skill or previous job, they're not allowed to restrict their job choices and must accept the minimum wage. It's almost as if: 'I'm down and you're keeping me down here'.
> (Adviser, Job Centre Plus, research jury day)

Conclusion

This chapter of the report has explored why a lifelong learning model of higher education is desirable, what it might look like and how it could be achieved. To ensure that a greater diversity of students are supported to succeed, a new model of higher education is required. Currently, the systems, even in institutions with a strong commitment to widening participation, are traditional and fixed; this is reinforced by the national reporting mechanisms and funding arrangements for institutions. Students are therefore not able to make the most of their higher education experiences. Most institutions have a long way to go:

> I think the university is a long way from being a genuine lifelong learning university. The university has a preoccupation with full-time study and it would require a major change in direction to be regarded as a lifelong learning institution – its shape would have to change significantly and the structure of funding *[from central government]* would have to facilitate this change.
> (Admissions officer)

6 Conclusion and recommendations

Conclusion: the real lifelong learners

Our research indicates that some working-class students who leave early see a value in university education and ultimately seek to return. It is crucial that the ladders out of poverty represented by universities lead somewhere meaningful for such working-class students and that they are supported to climb them. However, we believe that, in order to address the issue of working-class 'drop out' from universities, the concept and the debate need to be reframed.

While our research revealed that there are many ways in which institutions could improve their practice to retain those students who wish to stay, this amounts to tinkering with the system and does not address the fundamental issues that early withdrawal poses.

The research jury days revealed that the idea that working-class students are more likely to 'drop out' exists as a popular story producing significant negative effects on both students and the local area.

However, the interviews with students have shown that leaving university early was often a rational decision rather than a disastrous event and, moreover, that students planned to return to education at some later and more appropriate stage in their lives and make more informed choices of study.

Effectively, they were lifelong learners who were frustrated by an outmoded system. They learn a great deal from their university experience but, because they break the mould of three years' continuous study, it is devalued.

Universities, careers and employment services seemed to lack the ability to respond effectively to students who leave early, and the ethos of both employability and lifelong learning, which are strongly espoused in the UK, were not supported at a practical level.

We argue that, instead of constructing negative stories about working-class 'drop out', the emphasis at a policy and institutional level should be on creating more responsive and flexible systems that effectively incorporate universities into lifelong learning patterns and accommodate diverse students.

Institutional practices can certainly be improved to support those students who do want to remain on their courses but face difficulties and we have recommended ways in which this can be achieved. However, in our view, the current emphasis on retention diverts attention from the key issue of structural, systemic change.

The high rates of withdrawal among young working-class students are not a manifestation of their 'lack' but an indictment of the current rigid system that presents university as a once-only opportunity.

Working-class students who withdraw early in order to refocus and re-enter education are the real lifelong learners; institutions and policy makers have yet to catch up with them.

Recommendations

Government and policy makers

■ Recognise the potential benefits to some students of leaving early, in terms of making an informed decision and building their confidence, increasing their knowledge of which subjects they do/do not want to study and offering opportunities to pursue alternative pathways.

■ Place student withdrawal within a lifelong learning framework, which facilitates movement out of and into higher education throughout one's life.

■ Review the structure of HE and move towards creating a lifelong learning framework, including multiple entry and exit points and abandoning false distinctions between full- and part-time modes of study. This is an ambitious goal but a crucial one.

■ Remove financial penalties for HEIs and introduce payment for units studied rather than years of registration.

■ Allow longer periods of absence from HE, without having to withdraw students to enable them to extend their period of study to accommodate a wide range of circumstances.

■ Liaise with professional bodies, such as those in law, accountancy and medicine, to review the constraints they impose on HE delivery and curricula.

Institutions

Retaining students who might otherwise leave

■ Do not hide the fact that withdrawal is a possibility.

■ Recognise that many students have made incorrect course choices, so offer opportunities to change course, e.g. through guidance or a combined honours programme.

■ More emphasis should be given to providing meaningful information about individual subjects and courses, e.g. advice sessions on how to 'read' a prospectus could provide valuable guidance for both students and parents.

■ Introduce personal planning of 'non-traditional' pathways into and through HE.

■ Remove the distinction between full- and part-time mode, and make the possibility for less than full-time studying on all courses.

■ Alternatively, provide opportunities and support for students to change mode of study, e.g. from full to part-time and back again, to reduce their study load and accommodate changing circumstances.

■ Provide adequate financial support for students from low-income families.

■ Offer affordable and flexible childcare and other support services.

■ Provide for working-class students an appropriate curriculum that reflects and affirms their backgrounds.

■ Offer more proactive advice to students who are leaving, or are thinking of it, about both educational and employment options.

■ Develop stronger links between administrative staff dealing with withdrawal and teaching staff to ensure students at risk are referred for advice and guidance prior to withdrawal.

■ Provide training for personal tutors.

■ Have systems set in place to pick up on students at risk of withdrawal earlier in the process (e.g. missing tutorials/classes).

■ Develop pedagogy that supports integration, e.g. group work and peer support.

■ Improve and sustain student and staff awareness of existing forms of student support.

■ Develop more integrated and holistic approaches to student support (see Thomas *et al.*, 2002).

■ Integrate learning support within the curriculum.

■ Provide more student support that is targeted at particular disadvantaged groups.

■ Ensure data on current students and those who have withdrawn early is accurate.

Enabling students who have left to re-enter HE

■ Have multiple entry and exit points to/from HE.

■ Give credit to students for partially completing courses and instigate mechanisms to recognise this credit to facilitate re-entry to HE.

■ Follow up students who leave early to offer routes back into HE.

■ Set up local/regional structures to facilitate movement between institutions, based on credit already accumulated.

Supporting students who choose to leave

■ Do not perceive leaving early as a negative experience for all students and recognise that many want to come back in the future.

■ Explore the possibility of extending the careers service support to students who leave early.

■ Encourage employers to take on students during their studies, after part-completion and with alternative HE qualifications.

■ Develop links between employment agencies, student support and readmission processes to keep them in touch with the HEI.

Potential students

■ If possible identify the goal you are trying to reach and whether university is the best means of getting there.

■ Don't rush your choice of courses.

■ Try to find out exactly what is involved in the curriculum.

■ Try to identify your own strengths and weaknesses, and the kind of support you may need.

■ Learn where that support exists and seek it out.

Parents

■ Support your children to find out as much information as possible about courses, their requirements and what they will lead to.

■ Encourage your children to ask for the support and guidance they are entitled to.

■ Help them to explore flexible options such as a change of course and part-time study.

Schools and colleges

■ Encourage pupils to explore a range of options as well as university entry.

■ Focus on how to choose the appropriate course or subject.

Employers

■ Recognise the skills people have gained from entering and leaving HE.

Careers Service

■ Recognise students who withdraw early as a group who need your support.

■ Facilitate a careers discussion as part of the process of withdrawal.

Job Centre Plus

■ Recognise students who withdraw early as a distinct client group.

■ Encourage them to make use of the skills gained at university.

■ Do not channel them to low-waged jobs.

The media

■ Don't assume that leaving early is an easy decision or that it is necessarily negative.

■ Promote the implementation of lifelong learning within the context of HE – otherwise the UK may be left behind in the knowledge economy.

References

Bonin, S. (2004) 'Working-class student drop out trends in Canada', paper commissioned for this study and presented at 'Leaving early? International perspectives on working-class students' withdrawal', colloquium, Staffordshire University, 28 June

Carpenter, A. (2004) 'Social class, inequality and higher education in Ireland', paper commissioned for this study and presented at 'Leaving early? International perspectives on working-class students' withdrawal', colloquium, Staffordshire University, 28 June

Connor, H., Tyers, C., Modood, T. and Hillage, J. (2004) *Why the Difference? A Closer Look at Higher Education, Minority Ethnic Students and Graduates.* Research Report RR 552. London: DfES

Davies, R. and Elias, P. (2003) *Dropping Out: A Study of Early Leavers from Higher Education.* London: DfES

DfES (Department for Education and Skills) (2003a) *The Future of Higher Education.* White Paper. London: DfES

DfES (2003b) *Widening Participation in Higher Education.* London: DfES

Forsyth, A. and Furlong, A. (2003) *Losing out? Socioeconomic Disadvantage and Experience in Further and Higher Education.* Bristol: The Policy Press/JRF

Heagney, M. (2004) 'Dropping out in Australia: young students from low socio-economic backgrounds and non-completion', paper commissioned for this study and presented at 'Leaving early? International perspectives on working-class students' withdrawal', colloquium, Staffordshire University, 28 June

HEFCE (Higher Education Funding Council for England) (2005) *Young Participation in Higher Education.* Bristol: HEFCE

HESA (Higher Education Statistical Agency) (2004) *Performance Indicators in HE in the UK.* London: HESA

Heublein, U. (2004) 'Is there no way to the top for working-class children?', paper commissioned for this study and presented at 'Leaving early? International perspectives on working-class students' withdrawal', colloquium, Staffordshire University, 28 June

Johnes, J. and Taylor, J. (1991) 'Non-completion on a degree course and its effect on the subsequent experience of non-completers in the labour market', *Studies in Higher Education,* Vol. 16, No. 1, pp. 73–81

Johnston, V. (1997) 'Factors influencing progression in the first year of a degree programme: results from the first year student survey', student retention project, internal publication, Napier University, Edinburgh

Knighton, T. (2002) 'Postsecondary participation: the effects of parents' education and household income', *Education Quarterly Review,* Vol. 8, No. 3, pp. 25–32

Longden, B. (2003) 'Retention rates – renewed interest but whose interest is being served?', *Research Papers in Education,* Vol. 17, No. 1, pp. 3–29

Lynch, K. (1999) *Equality in Education.* Dublin: Gill and McMillan

NAO (National Audit Office) (2002) *Improving Student Achievement in the English Higher Education Sector.* London: The Stationery Office

Ozga, J. and Sukhnandan, L. (1997) *Undergraduate Non-completion in Higher Education in England.* Report 2. Bristol: HEFCE

Quinn, J. (2004) 'Understanding working-class "drop-out" from higher education through a socio-cultural lens: cultural narratives and local contexts', *International Studies in Sociology of Education,* Vol. 14, No. 1, pp. 57–75

Reay, D. and Ball, S. (1997) 'Spoilt for choice: the working-classes and education markets', *Oxford Review of Education,* Vol. 23, pp. 89–101

Schwartz, S. (2004) *Fair Admissions to Higher Education: Recommendations for Good Practice.* London: Admissions to HE Review, Steering Group

Scottish Executive (1999) *Social Justice – a Scotland Where Everyone Matters.* London: HMSO

Scottish Executive Enterprise and Lifelong Learning Committee (2002) 'Interim report on the Lifelong Learning Enquiry'

Skeggs, B. (1997) *Formations of Class and Gender.* London: Sage

Skeggs, B. (2004) *Class, Self, Culture.* London: Routledge

Smith, J. and Naylor, R.A. (2001) 'Dropping out of university: a statistical analysis of the probability of withdrawal for UK university students', *Journal of the Royal Statistical Society*, Vol. 164, No. 2, pp. 389–405

Tarleton, A. (2003) 'Wrong course, wrong time', *Guardian Unlimited*, 7 March

Thomas, L. (2002) 'Student retention in Higher Education: the role of institutional habitus', *Journal of Educational Policy*, Vol. 17, No. 4, pp. 423–32

Thomas, L., Quinn, J., Slack, K. and Casey, L. (2002) *Student Services: Effective Approaches to Retaining Students in Higher Education.* London: DfES

Thomas, E., and Quinn, J. (2003) *International Insights into Widening Participation.* Stoke-on-Trent: Institute for Access Studies, Staffordshire University

Times Higher Education Supplement (2005) 'Too cool for school: and its downhill from there', 25 February, p. 21

UUK (Universities UK) (2002) *Social Class and Participation: Good Practice in Widening Access to Higher Education.* London: UUK

Van Dyke, R. and Little, B. (2002) *Student Debt Project: Key Early Findings.* London: UUK

Vladacek-Hains, V., Divjak, B. and Horvatek, R. (2004) 'The importance of students' active participation and communication in colleges and universities and the possible impact on achievement', paper commissioned for this study and presented at 'Leaving early? International perspectives on working-class students' withdrawal', colloquium, Staffordshire University, 28 June

Yorke, M. (1997) *Undergraduate Non-completion in Higher Education in England.* Bristol: HEFCE